Secular Mann

A collection of Perry Mann essays

ISBN: 1514689650
ISBN 13: 9781514689653
Library of Congress Control Number: 2015910348
Createspace Independent Publishing Platform
North Charleston, South Carolina

Many thanks to Ann Ferrell Bowers and Chris Chanlett, both fellow admirers of Perry Mann. Ann first revealed the genius of Perry Mann to the general public in her book Mann and Nature.

PERRY MANN

Introduction by Julian Martin

"I AM THE VILLAGE ATHEIST," he told me shortly after we met. But evidently the voters of Summers County, West Virginia, didn't mind. They twice elected him prosecuting attorney and to the West Virginia legislature. His daughter has also been twice elected prosecuting attorney.

To Hinton in Summers County, I had made a pilgrimage to meet a man whose every op-ed in the Charleston Gazette caught and held my attention. I might say his idealism appealed to me, but Perry Mann isn't an idealist—he lived and appreciated an ideal life and based his essays on his life experience.

Perry Mann has been recognized in Robert Shetterly's Americans Who Tell the Truth. On the back cover of Mann and Nature: A Collection of Essays, compiled by Ann Farrell Bowers, Shetterly wrote these words of praise: "Working and living with nature have taught Perry Mann to respect the great web of life, which he believes is much stronger than any human activity. By abusing the earth and not realizing what we need to support the health of this web, he believes we are in danger of destroying ourselves and much of the earth's life forms with us. Not well known outside of his community in West Virginia, Perry Mann presents the importance of thousands of unheralded and critically important voices across our country."

Chris Chanlett honored his friend Perry Mann in the Charleston Gazette: "His sheer eloquence gives comfort to his faithful and challenge to his antagonists. He loves the arena of intellectual disputation and maintains a genial demeanor as he skewers fundamentalists. In over 1,500 columns he has sustained a radical critique of modern trends with a synthesis of liberal and conservative beliefs."

In her introduction to Mann and Nature, Ann Farrell Bowers paid this tribute to Perry Mann: "He was my high school English teacher, and his effect on me was profound. It has been said that it takes only a few good teachers to change a life forever, and he was mine."

You will find here Perry Mann's understanding of and expansion on thoughts, from among others, of Diogenes, Spinoza, Andre Sakharov, Tolstoy, Elie Wiesel, Jefferson, Henry George, Marx, Jesus, Toynbee, William Blake, Richard Dawkins, Copernicas, Darwin, Twain, A. E. Housman, Descarte, E. L. Doctorow, William James, and Pagans.

You will also find praise for famous composers and thoughts on such topics as free will and determinism, Christian fundamentalism, Moslem terrorism, hope without a heaven, homosexuality, World War II, George Bush, Iraq, Robert E. Lee, Washington and Lee University, socialism and capitalism.

These essays are from hundreds that Perry Mann wrote between 1999 and 2014. They were originally published in the Charleston Gazette and the Nicholas Chronicle, both West Virginia newspapers.

Contents

MANN on MANN

I was Shipped off to Live with My Grandparents

MY PARENTS WERE BOTH BORN and reared on subsistence farms, on farms that depended upon horse power and one that even had oxen power. My father at age 18 joined that great exodus in 1918, migrating to Charleston via the Chesapeake and Ohio Railway. Once he had employment, he married my mother, and they moved to Charleston and resided on Russell St. There I was born, and soon there were two other children.

During the Roaring Twenties things were roseate. Then came 1929 and then in 1933 the bank holiday. It was back to the land for me. Without employment, my father could not buy food for the table, and he had no land and sidewalks are sterile places for seeds. So I was shipped off to live with my grandparents who had land, and they harnessed my youth to help produce the food for the family.

I learned to plant corn, to thin corn, to plow corn, hoe corn, harvest corn, shuck corn, and feed corn to the animals that did their part in producing the food. I learned to cut hay, shock hay, barn hay, and feed hay in the darkness of winter evenings. I learned to plant wheat, cradle wheat, shock wheat, help the thrashing of wheat and the storing of it, the taking it to the mill, and the bringing it home flour. I learned to go to the forest in the fall with axe and crosscut saw to cut and haul in the winter wood, the only insurance against freezing to death and the only solace and security in dead of winter even with the downside of scorched shins and chilled backs.

I learned to harness horses and to use their power in all the ways horses could be used and enjoyed. I learned to milk cows, to shear sheep, to kill and butcher hogs, to hunt game, to swim, to fish, and to clean and eat all the meats caught, killed and butchered.

I experienced the memorable joy of sitting on the porch resting and facing the west after a day in the fields and a supper fit for a king—watching the sun set in all its glory. I enjoyed the moon and the stars, unalloyed with incandescent, every night when I prepared for bedtime. I'll never forget the long winter nights with its whistles of freeze and the times before the fireplace with family entranced by the embers of the backlog, warmed by the heat of the hot shambles of the fore logs, and sustained by the bucket of apples with paring knife and the popcorn popper.

And the meals: While the soup and bread lines lengthened in the cities, I sat down to three square meals a day. Breakfast often consisted of oatmeal and cream, cured ham, eggs, hot biscuits, home-churned butter, applesauce, and jellies. Dinner in summer was a table of vegetables, fried potatoes, hot bread, and in winter pork, beef, or lamb. Supper was as sufficient as dinner, summer and winter.

The apple house had shelves from floor to ceiling with Mason jars filled with meats and every vegetable and fruit grown on the farm. In the center were crates of apples and crocks of cider turning to vinegar. In the loft over the woodshed were bushels of walnuts, black and white, drying and, before the chestnut blight, there were buckets of chestnuts to peel, roast, and boil. In the meat house there were hams, shoulders and sides curing. Food for man and animals was canned, stored, cured, and preserved in quantities enough to survive the bitterest and longest winter.

Where Have the Horse Flies Gone?

ONCE, WHILE SITTING ON MY camp deck looking into the West for rain clouds, I noticed a horse fly on the railing, causing me to wonder what it was doing there and what kind of an existence it and its kin have had since the disappearance of nearly all the horses from these parts. What do they live on now that horses are gone from here and are concentrated in Lexington, Kentucky, and other horse capitals, where horse flies can expect little hospitality and much hostility? The sight of the fly did to me what smelling an apple or hearing a melody often does: it transported me to previous days and to the memories when the horse was at the top of the farmyard hierarchy.

Once upon a time horse flies had no trouble in this country finding a horse on which to engage in its parasitic practice. No farm was without horses. Horses did the heavy pulling, and always while they were so engaged, horse flies took the opportunity to alight at a point where neither the head nor the tail of the horse could disturb them. But the horses didn't take the landing of a horse fly on their back with equanimity.

The horses endured, more or less quietly, gnats in their ears and three-cornered flies taking a bite, but a horse fly was a fly of another size. And they pranced about a bit and did what they could to disturb the fly before it needled in and sucked its fill. Often when I saw that a horse fly had settled in on the back of a horse and had become absorbed in its sanguinary theft, I would slap it flat, feeling with the horse the relief.

The day on the farm, particularly in spring and summer, began with the rounding up of the horses and the harnessing them, for the horses pulled the plow, the disc, the harrow, the mowing machine, the rake, the sled, the wagon, the buggy, and just about everything that was too heavy for man to pull or move. To most farmers in this country in the Twenties and Thirties, horse power from horses was the only power except humans' backs and bones. There were few tractors, for there wasn't enough money to buy them. And my grandfather's farm was so steep and rocky, he couldn't have used one if he had had one.

I learned at an early age to chase the horses to the barn, where they entered the barn door always in the same order and always went to the same stall, just as people take the same place at the dinner table. I learned how to bridle them, harness them, hitch them to a sled that was runnered with hewn white oak secured with hickory pegs, and to drive them to the fields in spring to turn the ground.

I recall clearly the first time I went alone to a far field with horses and plow to turn three acres for corn. I was just twelve. The land was one piece of the few pieces on the farm that were not rocky so the plowing was relatively easy—no rocks to kick the plow out of the ground and jerk the horses and me about. I can recall the burnished blade cutting into the ground and laying it back, covering the field's growth, exposing the damp earth and occasionally turning up a mouse's nest, thereby ruining some best laid plans. At the end of the furrow, I could look back with satisfaction at the uniform rows of shining earth and when all the field was turned view a sea of upended soil, the first step toward an October of corn shocks and pumpkins.

At noon, I would unhitch the horses and mount one of them, hold the bridle of the other, and head for home for dinner. The horses knew that dinnertime was at hand, and they had the same renewed energy at the prospect of water and food I did. So, off they went with me astride at a slow run to the pond for water.

The pond was just below a spring and lay among trees. The place was cool on the hottest days. The horses would wade into the pond, triggering the jumps of a dozen frogs and causing sucking sounds as they pulled hooves from mud and a slurping sound as they drank. The dragon flies were everywhere, so delicate and so aeronautically agile. The frogs' heads would surface and survey the situation. But the horses were not long there and in a few minutes pulled out and headed for the barn and dinner, which consisted of a half dozen or so ears of corn apiece.

With the horses watered and fed, I headed for the house and the table. The noontime meal was not lunch. It was a full course of dishes. Biscuits and churned butter with transparent applesauce in spring were a daily treat. Wilted lettuce and onions another. Cured ham and canned sausage were available. Fried potatoes, canned beans, canned corn and tomatoes, pickles, jellies and jam were regulars at noon. Later in the summer when the garden came in, the noon table had on it every item touted in the seed catalogs. Meals in those days were the major returns and satisfactions from the work and the sweat of brows.

On the backside of my grandfather's bib overalls there was a worn ring at the waist, the result of reins tied behind his back when he plowed between rows of corn with a cultivating plow. His hands had to hold the plow handles so the reins were tied together and slipped over his head and shoulders to his waist. With the reins and the commands gee and haw, he maneuvered the horse and plow between row after row.

He taught me to cultivate with the horse. It was a frustrating job. The weather was always hot, the gnats were always swarming in my face, sweat bees stung at the slightest provocation, and the horse often had a mind of his own. Often the land was steep and rocky adding to the difficulty of keeping the plow between rows. And, of course, the horse flies were ever present tormenting the horse and making the job even harder.

Usually, at the end of the row, there were trees. The horse when he approached the trees, would hurry up, for he got relief from the gnats and flies and heat upon entering the brush and shade of the limbs, and so did I. Turning around and heading back in the next row was a slow and exasperating process. My will to leave the shade and begin another row was weak, and the horse's will to stay in the shade was strong. Thus, there was always the end-of-the-row crisis. However, it was better to cultivate than to hoe, for cultivating had an end but hoeing was interminable.

Then there was the mowing machine. I delighted in mowing the meadow with it. I always imaged that I was seated in a chariot warring against a sea of enemies that were cut down methodically. Grass quivered when the blade hit it and fell flat, a whole army annihilated in short order.

Next was the high-seated rake. It was light, and compared to the mowing machine it was a racer. The horses could almost trot as the machine made the rounds and the windrows grew until the field looked like some modern hairdos: rows of hair and bare scalp in between.

Those days, the people, the machines, and the horses are gone. The people lie moldering in family cemeteries, the machines are rusting or supporting mail boxes or resting in museums, and the horses for farming are confined to hippies, eccentrics, and sentimentalists. Man has had to adapt to sidewalks instead of walking cow paths, to air-conditioning instead of shade trees, to super markets instead of gardens, to automobiles instead of buggies, and to tractors instead of horses. The adaptation hasn't been easy, and much has been lost in the evolution from an agrarian to a cyber civilization.

Watching that horse fly on the railing, I reflected on its fate. Here was a creature fashioned by nature to live from blood of horses, and not a horse was within miles. It was forlorn. It was one of many species left behind by the motor and computer age. I felt a certain empathy for the horse fly and wondered how it lived. It can't get blood from a tractor, so it must reduce itself to getting blood from less princely animals than the horse losing thereby its dignity and standing. Its fate was not unlike that of the knights of yore who were reduced to playing chess rather than conquering castles, raiding its riches, and carrying away its maidens.

Math is a Mystery

RECENTLY I READ THIS HEADLINE: "Math rules cause worry at schools." It caught my attention because math has been a worrisome subject much of my life. I read further and learned that "starting next fall, all ninth-graders must be enrolled in algebra or a more advanced class, like geometry." I recalled at that moment having taken algebra in the ninth grade at Roosevelt Junior High School in 1936 and failing it. And I remembered how math had been a mystery to me in every course of it I had to take or took voluntarily. No subject or thing or event has contributed more to my lack of self-respect and confidence than has the mystery of math. Even Spanish was a mystery in junior high school. I failed it also. My parents had split, Depression had come, and I was so distracted by inner conflicts I couldn't focus for long on anything.

In high school, I had to take algebra again. I must have passed it but barely. In those days social promotions were common, and I was the recipient of a number of them. I took and just passed plane and solid geometry, and I took trigonometry. I knew not where I was in that course. Mr. Stedman, a kind man, gave me a D-. But he called me to his desk and gently and quietly told me that he was passing me, but that he knew and I knew that I didn't know much about trigonometry.

After graduating from Charleston High School in May, 1939, I enrolled in Morris Harvey College in the fall of that year. I was in the throes of first love, an absorbing, blissful, and woeful experience. Thus, at the end of the semester, I had to report to my father I had failed every course but physical education. It was a waste of his meager resources during the days of the Depression. But he was to live to learn that I could do better.

In the fall of 1941, I was employed at $65.00 a month as a board boy at Harris Upham & Co. I chalked up stock returns from tickertapes on a blackboard divided into panels of symbols for corporations and at end of the day typed the returns for the newspapers. I ate popcorn for lunch to save money, money that I was spending on piano and violin lessons. I had dreams of being a virtuoso pianist. But my dreams were interrupted with finality when the Japanese attacked Pearl Harbor.

In the army I was sent to army airways communication school where I was taught to use and repair radio equipment. I spent four years teaching, and using and repairing receivers and transmitters that were needed for point to point and ground to air communications, of which 18 months were spent in Algeria, Corsica, Italy and Tunisia. Math was not a problem. It was all the use of tech orders, schematics, tools, hands-on experience and trial and error.

On December 18, 1945, I was discharged honorably from the Army Air Corp at Fort Meade, Maryland. I had accumulated 48 months of GI Bill rights. I had become a different creature after four years in the army: I was integrated, and I could focus. I focused with the heat of the magnified sun on my learning the humanities and the knowledge to earn a living.

From another of Perry Mann's essays: "….I was the beneficiary of the GI bill and…I was lucky enough to take advantage of it, earning therefrom three degrees. The GI Bill made all the difference in my life, giving me self-employment, financial independence, philosophical orientation, time to myself, and access to nature, the last gift certainly being no less in value than all the others."

I entered Morris Harvey College in January, 1946. Since I had spent four years learning about and working with electronic equipment, I decided I would work toward a degree in electronics. But after taking a battery of tests, a professor advised that I would never make it in that field because of the math necessary to succeed in it. I was told that my strength was in languages. I have never received better advice or advice that was so critical in fashioning my future.

After a successful semester at Morris Harvey, I took a bus to Lexington, VA, where I had an appointment with Dean Gilliam to be interviewed. The dean had looked over my credentials and transcripts and he was not impressed. But he gave me a chance: If I would come to summer school and pass two courses with at least a C grade I could matriculate in the fall. I did better: I made a B in English and an A in history. Math had not come between me and my passion to learn, yet.

When I returned in the fall to W&L, I learned that there were required courses for a freshman, and I held my breath until I was told that I could take either algebra or Greek. I chose Greek before exhaling. I took two years of Greek and a year of Latin and made an A in every semester. I took French for two years and made A's. I took Anglo-Saxon, German, and Middle English and aced them all. I took many English courses, history, philosophy, biology, and religion. I gorged gloriously on the humanities. In fact, I graduated from W&L summa cum laude and was elected to Phi Beta Kappa in my junior year. I was also chosen to be a candidate for a Rhodes Scholarship. I hitched-hiked to Richmond, VA, for the interview. I never got to Oxford. If I had, I might have had to face math.

After graduating and while teaching in a high school, I took at night a course in algebra. I wanted to pass algebra just to prove that I could. I failed. I was an A student in languages but an F student in mathematics. It was because of my genes, because of my innate makeup.

My father was mathematical. My mother was verbal. I inherited my mother's verbal genes. I am handicapped by my lack of mathematical intelligence. There is no teacher in the land who can make me a successful student in mathematics even if I put forth a Herculean effort. If I had had to vault the bar of math in order to be where I am, I would not be where I am. I might not have succeeded at W&L.

Those who insist a student succeed in math in order to have a degree need to consider every child is not born with the inbred intellect to cope with math but may have the inborn intellect to succeed with languages. There is an equal need in the world for those who can figure and for those who can write. For curriculum makers to require that all students take and pass four years of math, including algebra and its sisters, is to assure that many students will fail, dropout, and forever feel inadequate.

Wheat Harvest in the Thirties

THIS TIME OF YEAR ON the farm in the Thirties was time to harvest wheat. It seemed esthetically a shame to harvest a field of gold that undulated from the winds' caresses not unlike the waves of seas. But the grain was ripe and had to be harvested, or it would go to ruin.

In my early teens my grandfather had taught me the skill of handling and using a scythe. There is an art to cutting with one. I used to take a swath and my grandfather would lead the way with a swath. It was learning that could be transferred to the use of a cradle, the instrument in those days that was used to cut wheat.

The cradle was a scythe with an enlarged blade. It had four or five fingers of wood attached to it parallel to the blade. When the cradler cut a swath, the scythe blade cut the grain at ground level, and the fingers gathered the cut wheat as the cradler completed his swing. Then, the cradler parked the cradle on the thigh of his left leg, reached for the gathered wheat, and dropped the bundle to the ground. Behind came one who gathered the bundles until they were the size to tie with strands of wheat and left to become part of wheat stack or shock later.

There was a rhythm to the use of the cradle: the swing to cut the swath, the parking the cradle on the thigh, the gathering the cut wheat, and the dropping of it behind for the bundler. It was swing, park, gather, drop, and return to beginning of the next stroke of the cradle hour after hour until the field was stubble and shocks.

Though I was still in my middle teens, my grandfather gave me the job of cradler. I felt important. Though the going wage for field work was ten cents an hour, cradlers were paid fifteen cents an hour. I was not paid in cash; I cradled for my bed and keep, but I knew the difference in pay and swelled somewhat. But the work was hard, arduous, and exhausting. I cradled ten hours with breaks and water from a jug. At night I couldn't quit cradling. I cradled in my sleep and often awoke tired from it.

At the end of the day the bundles had to be gathered and shocked and capped to shed rain. One year rain came and came again and again until the wheat in the caps sprouted. That wheat was lost, but the wheat covered survived and went into the thrashing machine that separated wheat from straw and chaff.

Taking view of that part of the wheat field that was now stubble and shocks of wheat was to a cradler a pretty sight, a satisfying scene. Here was bread and feed for humans and animals. It was that without which life on the farm would have been poor indeed.

My grandfather hired an adult neighbor to tie behind me. He had no experience with a cradling, but he asked my grandfather if he could try the cradle. He felt somewhat degraded tying bundles behind a kid. He took the cradle and went at the work with enthusiasm, but he made a mistake. When on a swing he gathered the wheat from the fingers, he grabbed the blade and cut himself. That ended the neighbor's employment in the wheat harvest. I went back as cradler.

After the shocks had seasoned some in the summer sun, it was time to haul the shocks to the barn. The horses were rounded up, harnessed, hitched to sled or wagon, and reined to the wheat field. The shocks were stacked on the vehicle and hauled to the barn to be stored until the thrashing machine came.

The coming of the thrashing machine was always an exciting time. The machine would come early with its crew to a farm and thrash, then to the next farm, and at noon it would come to a farm prepared for its coming and for the feeding the crew and all the other men and women involved in the festival.

But first there was the thrashing. The bundles were hauled from barn to one end of the thrashing machine, which had been steadied and hooked by belt to a tractor. When all was ready, the tractor would start, and the machine would groan and shake. Bundles entered one end, and chaff exited the other end. In the middle on the side, the golden grain spouted into half bushel buckets. I was one of them there to sack the grain from the buckets.

The women had congregated at the appointed place for dinner, not lunch, but dinner and a dinner with many courses, many entrees, abundances of vegetables, and endless desserts. The men came and prepared for the feast by going to the spring house and drinking dipper after dipper of cool, quenching spring water. I often would throw a dipper or two on my head to help relieve the itch of chaff and dust, and so did my buddies. Then we went to the washstand on the porch of the neighbor's house to wash up. Basins of rain water from rain barrel and soap and towels were there to clean off the sweat and dirt of thrashing.

Then, shifts of workers took seats around the dining room table and were served by the women. One can imagine the joy and festivity of such an occasion. How happy were the men to be doing the work so essential to life and doing it with other men and women who were their neighbors and helpers and there to assure sustenance and enjoy fellowship. And how happy were the men to eat with yearning appetites and happy were the women to provide for them and note the success of their cooking skills.

The thrashing and dining done, the crew hitched the tractor to the machine and with a part of the wheat as their pay departed.

The women cleaned up after the feast, and the men followed the machine and crew to the next farm. Then the sun set and there was to come another day and another harvest. So was the calendar of events and the way of life for the Mountaineers in the Thirties.

My Ties to Chesapeake and Ohio Railway

ABOUT 1870 THE C&O HAD built its railroad to Talcott, WV. It had followed the Greenbrier River from Ronceverte. But at Talcott the river ran into Big Bend Mountain and had to make a sharp left turn and follow at the base of the mountain for 15 miles just to get to the other side of the mountain which was only a mile or so as the crow flies from the Talcott side. Thus, rather than build 15 miles of railroad along the river around the mountain, the C&O dug the Big Bend Tunnel which was just a mile and a quarter in length. Helping to cut through the mountain was a steel-driving man named John Henry who became a legend that is well-known.

In 1883, my grandfather had about ninety acres surveyed on top of Big Bend which he bought from the Rollyson family. He built his house there and raised with my grandmother five children to adulthood. My father was one of them. My mother's father had a few hundred acres of bottom land bordering the river where the railroad would have gone had no tunnel been constructed. My father courted my mother, and they married and honeymooned in Washington D.C., having traveled there by the C&O Railway.

My father's prospects in Summers County were not promising. WW I had just ended, and there was work in Charleston, WV. He took his bride and boarded the train at Hinton and left Summers County and never returned except for visits via the C&O and later by auto. He acquired a house on Russell St. and with his bride set up housekeeping. Children came. I was first born March 12, 1921. At the birth with my mother were her mother and my father's sister. They had come to Charleston on the C&O and returned home on the train. When my sister came two years later, my aunt came to help my mother through the birth, and she took me with her to the farm by train.

I was the first male grandchild, and I was treated as a prince by my grandparents and spinster aunt. Even at that early age I began to love the place. I had a dog and cat. I fed chickens with my grandmother. My grandfather would come in from the fields with something in his pocket and ask me to reach in to see what it was. Once I remember well it was a rabbit so tiny it would fit in a teacup. I watched my aunt milk cows, I watched my grandfather slop the hogs, and I saw meadows and woodlands and creeks and sky and clouds and at night the heavens in all their glory unadulterated with the light of any other thing but maybe lightning bugs. Once my grandmother took me to the chicken house to a setting hen's nest. She lifted the hen in spite of her protests and revealed a nest full of fuzzy chicks. The consequence of this love was that I was on that farm with them every chance I had throughout my early life. And the way I got there was, you guessed it, the C&O Railway.

During the Depression, I spent many months and years with my grandparents. I used to beg my parents for the $1.93 which was the fare from Charleston to Hinton on what else but the C&O Railway. I never had more than the fare. When the porter came through hawking coffee and ham sandwiches, I had belly rumbles over the thought of a ham sandwich. But the sandwich, which was two thick slices of bread between which was a sump-tuous slice of ham, was 25 cents. I had not a nickel on me. I was happy when he went to the next car. The yearn for that sandwich somewhat subsided.

I spent at the farm every Thanksgiving, every Christmas, and every Easter Holiday I could get the $1.93. Also, matters got so bad at home that I went to live with my grandparents year around. It was an education one could not receive any other way or place. I learned the basics and realities of life. I helped to prepare soil for seeds, to cultivate them, to harvest them and to watch the process of tabling them. I watched my grandmother choose a chicken for the pot and see that it got there. I have been there and helped in November to kill the hogs, butcher them, carve out the hams and shoulder, grind the pieces to sausage, and watch my grandmother in inclement weather squatting to clean intestines for soap making. I have helped to shear sheep for their wool and to clip the tails of lambs and castrate calves and pigs. That is I have worked at the bottom of the economic mountain, the top of which are those players who gamble with the wealth that the bottom has produced just as the Saturday-night kind role dice to gain by luck.

In December of 1941, I boarded a New York Central car to be transported to Columbus, Ohio, where I was inducted into the Army Air Corp. From there by train I was transported to Jefferson Barracks, Missouri. Months later I hitchhiked from St. Louis to Charleston. Then back to the C&O for a ride to Detroit and some basic training, after which I boarded a C&O train to be carried to Newport News, Virginia, to become one of hundreds on a troopship. The train passed through Charleston on the way and stopped there in the middle of the night. I had my last sight of my hometown for a while. In December, 1945, I entrained the C&O at Union Station, Washington, D.C. for a transport to Charleston and home.

Incidentally, while going through my grandfather's papers years after the war, I discovered a document showing that he had sold to the C&O Railway 18 chestnut oak railroad ties he had hewn with a broadax. The farm he got from the Rollyson folk was rocky but also tree wealthy.

Today, the C&O tracks are a football-field distance from my front door. I hear the trains often and see the coal trains going east full and going west empty. And I hear Amtrack blow its horn from time to time. The Fast Flying Virginia and the George Washington, C&O's super passenger trains, are memories come alive on Railroad Days.

Farm Sundays in FDR Days

Sunday began on Saturday. It was the day that my grandmother surveyed her chicken flock and decided which one of them would be in the pot for Sunday dinner. She would gather up her apron into a container, pour a handful of cracked corn into it, walk into the chicken yard, and call chick, chick, chick. The henhouse gang was soon at her feet pecking corn. She would maneuver to be above the chosen victim; in a flash she would have the chicken by the legs. She would secure the wings and feet, go to the chopping block, and with an ax sever its head. Then she would scald, pluck, eviscerate, and make it pot or skillet ready.

Sunday was a day of rest, no work except what had to be done. Cows were milked, pigs were fed, and dog and cat fed. Breakfast was prepared and eaten. The rest was mostly for males. The women had to prepare the biggest meal of the week: Sunday dinner. Much was done early toward preparing that meal because church attendance was a must.

My grandfather sang in the choir. He had a hymnal with shaped notes. The shape of the note determined it musical value. He also had a tuning fork. He would dress early while the women rushed about doing necessary chores and would sit on the porch in a split bottom, strike his tuning fork on the banister, and sing quietly to himself. He was practicing for his choir responsibilities.

My grandparents had a closet about the size of a telephone booth. It contained their Sunday best which wasn't worn except on Sundays and at funerals. Someone always had to tie my grandfather's tie. Aunt Sadie did it for years. I also helped to tie it when I learned how. Grandmother dressed in black with some lace here and there and flat-heeled shoes. Spike heels would not do on country roads. Before leaving for church, my grandmother, whose only income was from the sale of eggs, would call me into her bedroom and take from a purse a dime for me to contribute to the collection at church.

It was time now to depart for church. It was a half mile walk, but all walked. In the early years the walk was a country road, dust in summer and mud in winter. Later a hard surface road was built not far from the house and gave easier access to the church. The church was the Mt. Pisgah Methodist.

It was a box of a steepled church with wooden benches, a wood-fired stove on either side, a pulpit and a wrap-around railing with a cushioned runner for the sinners to kneel on when confessing sins or converting. My aunt played the organ and grandfather sat with the choir. Grandmother had her friends. I got with my buddies. Sunday was about the only day my buddies and I got to be together in summer months with the exception of a fishing expedition in the Greenbrier on some holidays.

Before preaching, there was Sunday school. The congregation was divided into four groups according to age. Granddad and grandmother sat in one corner of the church with the oldsters, Aunt Sadie taught a class of youth and I sat with Punk, my buddy, with the teen group taught by Uncle John Carden, who was my mother's uncle and was married to my grandfather's sister. We always received literature that had Jesus' picture on it and was inscribed with Scripture. The Scripture was the teaching theme for the day.

After a break outside and lots of talk, the call came to re-convene for preaching. First there was a hymn or two. One I can hear now: "I come to the garden alone while the dew is still on the roses and the voice I hear falling on my ear…" Then, there was the collection and after another hymn the sermon. Different preachers had different styles. But most were passionate and bombastic. Hell and Heaven were real. The former for the bad and latter for the good—good being church going believers. Usually there was a call to come forward to the altar to confess sins. To accompany this call the choir always gave forth with a hymn with these words sung over and over: "Almost Persuaded." Once, after the call to come had gone long sans any sinner coming forth, I suggested to Punk that we go forward for the fun of it and to accommodate the preacher. We did and went to the kneeling place and had an intimate conversation with the preacher.

Church over, there was the collection of congregants outside to determine who would have dinner with whom. Always on Sunday after church someone went with someone else to have dinner. My choice for dinner guest was often my buddy. Punk and I were inseparable. It was an irritant to the adults. But we were alike, and our thinking and genetic composition were close. So, Punk came home with me to have helpings of the chicken grandma had sacrificed on Saturday for the meal on Sunday.

Punk's family was a victim of the Depression. His father lost his job and had no other prospects than to come to the home of his widowed sister. She had a farm that adjoined my grandfather's farm. There were Lonnie, Bessie, and five children, Punk being one of them. They had no cows or horses, so they had to exchange man-power for horse-power. Their lot was tough. So when Punk came to eat with me, he had as many glasses of milk as he dared ask for. And when I ate at his house, I discovered when I lifted my knife for butter to spread on my bread; there was no butter on the table.

After dinner we were free, but we had to abide by the Old Testament. We could not do anything forbidden by it. But Punk and I were pagans. We knew that in Hinton there was a theatre where motion pictures were presented and we had the money for admission. So we went to the highway and hitchhiked to Hinton to see "Dark Victory" starring Bette Davis after which we had the problem of getting back to Mt Pisgah before the evening service so that our sin would not be discovered. We hitchhiked and were successful. We were in church with innocence writ all over us for the evening service.

Punk and His brother marched across Europe and were those who helped to make possible the victory of the Allies over the Nazis and who survived to come home to the land of their fathers. I too tagged along and visited many places in North Africa and Europe: Italy, Corsica, France, Algeria, and Tunisia. And, I came home to celebrate with Punk. I later did his will and attended his funeral.

Music in My Life

IN HIGH SCHOOL, I WAS an introvert, a painfully self-conscious teen, a non-athlete, a poor student, socially a nobody, a punching bag for bullies and just a nice-kid to the girls. My parents divorced when I was 12, which separation wounded home life and exacerbated the pain of the Depression, during which my father's bank closed forever after the Bank Holiday. I sought relief wherever I could find it. I became an addicted listener of the radio, from which I learned that on Sundays there was a classical program of music played by the Philadelphia or New York Philharmonic orchestra.

At first it was the Strauss waltzes that lifted my spirits. Then I become acquainted with the works of other popular classic composers: De Falla, Grieg, Tchaikovsky, Saint Saens, Berlioz, Korsakov, Ravel, Rossini, Debussy, and many others. Eventually I discovered Bach, Beethoven and Brahms and have in memory every one of their major works. Also, I discovered nearly all the great composers and could recognize their respective compositions. And every composition that on first hearing lifted me out of myself into a soaring bliss, I remember where I was when I heard it.

Beethoven Fifth Symphony I heard the first time on a Sunday prior to Pearl Harbor performed by the Philadelphia Philharmonic. I remember the tiptoeing that foreshadows the

Grand Crescendo and the swelling of the music, louder and louder and reaching a point where it falls on itself and cascades downward leaving one having experienced the excitement and delight of an emotional climax.

I enlisted in the army in 1941 and was sent to many camps and cities. In Detroit I went to a USO where there were sound-proof booths for soldiers to listen to classical music. It was in one of these booths that I first heard Beethoven's Third Symphony or "Eroica." I couldn't keep from directing the orchestra. I was hooked at first hearing by the great themes, the energy and optimism, and fist-shaking defiance. Beethoven had Fate by the throat and throttled it.

One of the most memorable introductions to a great classic happened in Sioux Falls, South Dakota. I was there as an instructor in radio maintenance. I met a woman instructor and fell in love. She loved classical music too. So I bought an old tabletop radio for a speaker and bought a turntable and pickup for 78 rpm records. I united electronically the two and had a record player which I took to her apartment. Among the albums I bought was Beethoven's violin concerto. We listened to it together in the fall of 1943. Whenever I hear that concerto, I remember that afternoon and remember with acute nostalgia Esther Wiseheart and the glorious fall weather of South Dakota.

While stationed in Chicago, I was present in many concerts given by the Chicago Symphony. Admission for a soldier was just a quarter. I had the exciting experience of hearing Sergei Rachmaninov play his Rhapsody on a Theme of Paganini. The audience stood up and applauded when he came on stage.

Overseas I was stationed on Corsica. I lived in a tent and slept on a bunk with a radio at my head. I listened to the BBC from London nightly, and I heard hours of classical music. It was on one of those nights that I heard Wagner's love music from Tristan and Isolde. What an experience! The music soars slowly and pleasurably and then mounts, culminating in the sweet, throbbing throes of intimacy and falls off precipitously into a delightful languor.

Home from the service, I was with my future wife at a swimming hole on the Jackson River in Virginia. A friend of hers had a portable radio playing, and amid all the distractions, I began to hear classical music. I listened and I couldn't get away from it. The music was the last movement of Schubert's 9th Symphony. The music was galloping with shouts of brass and pounds of drums and a theme that haunted. I discovered that day the best of Schubert, and he has been a companion of mine ever since. I also discovered years later his inimitable and glorious Trout Quintet.

There was a time when I first heard Brahms 1st and 2nd piano concertos. It was long ago, but I have listened to them over and over. They are wonderful works of art. In recent years I have discovered Saint Saens' piano concertos, his symphonies, and other works. I have listened to Sibelius' 2nd symphony. Whenever I hear it, I say to myself: "This is a cry in dead of winter of a Finlander for the warmth of the south of Italy."

Why I discovered classical music and immediately found great pleasure in it is a mystery. My grandparents never heard of Bach, Beethoven and Brahms, much less Wagner, Mahler, Vivaldi, Haydn, Mozart, and many others. My father never heard of them, and if my mother heard of them, she never mentioned them to me. But that I did discover classical music and learn to appreciate it has been one of the joys of my life.

One day after I returned from the war, I got a call from California. It was Esther Wiseheart. She told me that she had married and moved west. She wished to know what I wanted for the record player and records that I left with her when I went overseas. I mentioned a nominal amount. And she said: "Perry, you were always generous. Thanks."

Algeria, World War II

IN 1941, I WAS TWENTY. I was a high school graduate but a socially promoted one, specifically in trigonometry. I hadn't been out of the state but once and that to Virginia. I was innocent as to the ways of the world. But on December 12, 1941, I joined the Army Air Corp and after service in the states, I eventually arrived in Algiers, Algeria. There my innocence ended.

What I saw and learned there opened my eyes and mind to the evils of colonialism and in retrospect revealed to me the origins and causes of what has been the history in Algeria and the rest of the Middle East since.

First I noticed the abysmal and appalling poverty of the Arabs, or WOGs[1], the epithet used by the British. Many lived in shacks with earthen floors and mud-brick walls with ragged children everywhere, some of whom were blind. A look at their water supply would make one gag. In Algiers many storefront entrances were at night beds for the homeless. Many Arab males had fashioned pants from barrack's bags, the drawstrings of which served as belts. Arab women were mostly absent except those who had westernized and those who had become whores.

One night while abed in my quarters, which were attached to a radio communication facility, I saw, guarding the area, black Senegalese soldiers in French uniforms doing their prayers to

---

1 Western Oriented Gentleman

Allah, which prostrations they would do day and night with regularity. I learned from the prayers that I was in a Muslim world, but a world ruled by Christians, who were a wee minority. This fact was evident everywhere.

Thievery by the Arabs was rampant and skilled. One soldier lost his shoes while asleep or drunk. The thief cut his laces with a razor blade and removed them. It was reported that on the airbase theft became such a problem that at night a gunner sat in a bomber turret with a view of the field, and when lights flooded the field, anyone in sight was shot. I was with a patrol at night when a WOG was caught. Rather than go to the trouble of incarcerating him, a British sergeant suggested that we look the other way, and when he ran, he would kill him. The captive ran as expected, and a hail of lead followed him. But he apparently knew to run and fall and then run again. He disappeared into the dark.

I had the responsibility of maintaining a radio-directional facility a mile or so from the airfield. Part of the responsibility was to maintain a field-phone connection from the field to the facility. As certain as I laid a line from the field to the facility, Arabs would take it up. There was a black market for most anything they could steal. Cigarettes were a medium of exchange.

A WOG attacked a British soldier in a nightclub. The British dragged the Arab outside and beat him either to death or near to death. WOGs were inferior humans and were treated that way. Americans hadn't become so hardened by the realities of occupation and colonialism as they are today as manifested by shocking instances of killing, torture, and rape in Iraq; and they were more generous and charitable toward the Arabs. Americans were generally treated with respect.

Three soldiers and I were given the detail of guarding three freight cars of radio equipment on a train that was going from Algiers to Biskra, an oasis and resort in the Sahara desert where the Allies had an airfield. The train trip took a week. The experience of the ride is another story. What I remember relative to conditions today is that at every stop at a station, WOGs would by the dozens race to the train to find a place to hang on, and just as soon as they found a place, a French conductor with a big stick would began beating them with bureaucratic zeal until they retreated. This episode was repeated at every stop.

Once, the train passed through a tunnel. I was riding on a platform at the end of a car, and I nearly suffocated from the heat and smoke before the train exited the tunnel. I was soot covered, head to toe. When the train made a stop in Constantine, a city named after the Emperor and located in the Atlas Mountains, I went to find water to cleanse myself. I saw a military base with an Arab guard at the gate. With the French word douche and with my fingers imitating water showering my head, I was able to communicate to him. He understood and took me to a pipe arising from the parade ground with a spigot attached. The water was cold, and it was chilly in late October in the Atlas Mountains. This was where the Arab soldiers showered and washed. I indicated that I wanted hot water. The Arab then took me to a French officer who took me to his office and introduced me to his personal shower, hot water and all.

One day I was walking somewhere near the airfield at Biskra when I saw coming toward me a young Arab in military uniform. As he neared, I could see that he had been shot up pretty badly and had recovered enough to be discharged and sent home. I learned from him with my bit of French and his bit of English he had been wounded somewhere in the fighting in Europe and was on his way to his family and home. To this day, I cannot get out of my mind the difference between what that boy experienced in the war and what I experienced and what he gave and received and what I gave and received. His wounds would impair him for the rest of this life, and he came home to a mud hut and little else for his service and sacrifice.

The WOGs of Algeria, as I remember, were the serfs, and the French and British and Americans were the lords. The Arabs, I suspect, had little to hang on to but Allah and His promise of the rewards of Paradise. It may be that the broken soldier I met had children, and they had children, all of them knew the history of their ill treatment and also all believed in Allah and his reward of Paradise. These are the terrorists of today. The wrongs the West sowed are now the harvest of evil it reaps. Nations, just as people, are not immune to Fate's judgments and its punishments for their errors and evils.

General Robert E. Lee Insurance Co., Inc.

IN JUNE, 1945, HOME FROM the war with four years of G I Bill credit, I went to Lexington, Va., for an interview with Dean Gilliam, hoping as a result to enter Washington and Lee University in the fall. My high school credentials were poor; so the dean allowed me a provisional entry, the provision being I do at least C work in two summer school courses beginning in July. I succeeded, and in the fall I became a W&L under-graduate.

At the first convening of the student body, Francis Pendleton Gaines, president and orator extraordinaire, spoke to the student body at some length regarding the history of the institution. He reminded the students that George Washington had given Chesapeake and Ohio canal stock of a value of $50,000 to endow the institution long ago but that it was still paying part of their tuition.

Then he spoke about Robert E. Lee. He talked his way through the agony of secession, the failure of the Peninsular Campaign, the carnage of Fredericksburg, the defeat at Gettysburg, the awful costs of Cold Harbor, the breakout at Petersburg, and finally of the retreat to Appomattox and the surrender there to General Grant.

He was a spellbinder, and he had even the most cynical students moved and receptive and ready for more. He paused a bit and continued with an event that happened after the surrender when General Lee on Traveler was returning from Appomattox to Richmond. The word was out that Lee was coming and the roadway was lined with people hoping to see the great man as he passed. It was a sad journey: the cause was lost; the South was in ruins; her youth decimated and her veterans exhausted and impoverish. As Lee came to a small village, a young mother, widowed by war, with babe in arms hurried to the roadside, went up to the General, and pleaded: "General Lee, tell me something to tell my child." Lee stopped, looked at the mother and replied, "Teach him to deny himself."

At this moment the Southern boys were ready to sing Dixie and pledge the South would rise again. President Gaines had me choked up and wet of eye. I had never listened to a man with such oratorical powers, save Winston Churchill. It was an unforgettable moment for me. And I was transfixed as he continued.

Lee, who had lost not only a war but his property and his rank and office, was offered aid and positions from many quarters and generalships from European powers. But he declined them and accepted the presidency of struggling Washington College in Lexington, Va., where he lived and worked the remaining days of his life and where he lies buried beneath the edifice named for him: Lee Chapel. The institution that he revived added his name to become Washington and Lee.

President Gaines may have told the following story, which I have just recently come across, but if he did I do not remember it. But it is a story America should know and consider in the context of how ready celebrities are to prostitute themselves these days by selling their name and face for a price, and a big price at that.

Lee, broke and unemployed, was offered by a Yankee insurance company $50,000 (a million today) to use his name. Lee's response was chillingly succinct and bluntly unequivocal: "I cannot consent to receive pay for services I do not render."

How quaintly odd, strange, antediluvian, perverse, parochial was Lee's rejection of such an offer, when one considers consenting to receive pay for no services rendered is a way of life today. What would Lee have thought of a war hero and an ex-senator who would sell his fame and honors in order get big money hawking a drug that provides impotent men with the necessary readiness to perform sexually? Or of men who are adept at tossing a ball through a hoop selling their fame for $20 million a year to sell sneakers? Or of the hundreds of people with some notoriety that wear ads on their clothing, cars, and anywhere else for big money?

Another question is what kind of people would offer Robert E. Lee $50,000 for his name in order to exploit it and his reputation and renown for profit? Who would have the effrontery, the insensitivity, the mania for money to even request the use of his name much less to use it in advertisements if consent had been forthcoming? Here is a man who at the moment of the request had shortly before surrendered his sword and signed a pact accepting defeat with his adversary; lost a war upon which the whole of the South had risked everything to win; and had on his mind the deaths in vain of hundreds of thousands of young men and the vast destruction of the South from Chattanooga to Savannah, from Texas to Virginia. And some men in a big city of the North, dreaming prospects, have this meretricious epiphany: Just think what this insurance company could do with a name like General Robert E. Lee Insurance Co., Inc. Why his name is known and respected the world around. We could sell angels life insurance with a name like that.

I can conjure up some ads that they had in mind if Lee had the passion for profit these men had and that their heirs, successors and assigns have rabidly at this very hour: "If you suffer a Gettysburg be assured if you have a policy with the General Robert E. Lee Insurance Co. Inc." Or "Appomattox is not the end if you have a General Lee policy." And if the company were alive today, one could be certain that he would be, with numbing repetition, reminded that life is short and unpredictable and that young matrons with children never know when the bread winner may fall at the wall at Fredericksburg, so to speak.

In that summer of 1945, I sat in class with Robert E. Lee IV. It meant something to me to be so near history, so near the son of the son of the son of the son of the man who gave his name to the school I was attending and who left a legacy that brings tears to the romantic and idealistic. I don't know where Robert IV is, but I hope he is not an agent for an insurance company that has incorporated the name of his illustrious ancestor. It would be too much to bear in this world so filled with entrepreneurs with the shamelessness of those who tried to buy Robert E. Lee's name and character.

Notorious Nonsequitur

I AM THE FATHER OF a gay son. Therefore, I have standing to defend homosexuals in the court of controversy regarding same-sex marriage and the whole of the straight-gay argument. Based on that credential and common sense, I take issue with "Catholic hierarchy supports preserving definition of marriage," which publication appeared in the March 4th edition of the Nicholas Chronicle. [Nicholas County, West Virginia]

First and foremost, it is beyond argument, among scientists and reasonable thinkers, that sexual orientation is not a matter of choice but is a matter of nature and nurture, both of which factors determine perforce the character of every individual. No man or woman would choose freely to be sexually attracted to the same sex in a world where most heterosexuals believe such orientation is an abomination in God's eyes and is an abomination in their eyes.

A homophobe should ask himself: When was I presented with the choice of being gay or straight, and why did I choose to be straight instead of gay? No one can say he remembers making such a choice. Because no one chooses. One just is.

No one in his right mind would choose to be gay in a world that looks upon homosexuality as an evil and upon gays as fair game to taunt, to mock, to heckle, and even to stomp just because of an orientation over which they have no control. To believe that gays choose to be gay is a belief embraced to justify the natural antipathy that heterosexuals have for homosexuals.

St. Paul was not immune to such antipathy and thus expressed his homophobia in a letter that has since given his prejudice the status of the word of God, when in fact it was the word of a man. No man who is fully acquainted with the Bible and the critical scholarship concerning it and who is in command of his fantasies believes that the Bible's authors were other than ordinary men with all the good and bad characteristics of Adam's heirs. Man cites man when he cites Scripture—a mischievous circumlocution that inspires homophobia.

Catholics believe: "Marriage, as instituted by God, is a faithful, exclusive, lifelong union of a man and woman joined in an intimate community of life and love. The reality of marriage between one man and one woman is written in the very nature of man and woman as they came from the hand of the creator." When and how did God institute marriage? Man and woman have been mating, conceiving children and caring for their welfare for millions of years, eons before the present conception of God was envisioned and eons before the sacrament of marriage was conceived by a man-made and worldly religious entity. Otherwise, there would be no human beings and no church.

The quoted statement in the previous paragraph would be just as correct if, wherever man and woman appears same-sex partners were to appear. It would be just as correct because, if God made heterosexuals, he also made gays. That is, He did if gays are gay as a result of nature and nurture and not choice. And that gays have no choice as to their sexual orientation is, in my mind, beyond question, just as it is clear in my mind man has no free choice in any aspect of his being or his actions. Philosophers and scientists have argued for centuries free will is an illusion.

Only man and woman can by sexual union create children, and thus only man and woman should be able to marry, contend

Catholics. Priests marry God and dedicate themselves to celibacy. No children can come from such a union. But the church blesses their union, and priests undoubtedly take spiritual comfort from such a union. Many heterosexual men and women marry, some intending never to have children and some intending to have them but who never conceive children, and yet they live a lifetime together then bemoan the loss of a partner. Gays wish to marry to have the same comfort that priests and childless couples have.

Bishop Schmitt is quoted: "God took the reality of marriage, which He created, and made a witness and a testimony of His love for the world." This is romantic mythology and theological fantasy and has little reason or reality in it. The quote is more realistically stated in this manner: Nature created life and invented sex as a means to perpetuate it. She made male and female, adapting them and conditioning them in such a manner that they tend lovingly to cohabit and procreate. Love is a natural force created by nature to assure the union of man and woman. It is also a force that for reasons known only to nature causes some men to love men and some women to love women.

If marriage and sexual orientation originated with God or nature, then whatever one's orientation, he or she should not be denied the right to enter into a relationship sanctioned by the church and recognized by the state and should have all the rights and privileges pertaining thereto. If churches wish to wash their hands of same-sex marriage, they have the option. But they should not try to obstruct or prevent civil marriage as an option for gays on the ground that God would object and that the sacredness of traditional marriage is threatened by it. The union of man and woman is no more sacred than the union of bluebirds, and a homosexual union is no more a threat to a heterosexual union than the union of bluebirds is to the marriage of either of them.

It's a notorious nonsequitur to premise on Scripture one's argument that marriage is God's creation, that homosexuals are an abomination to God and that therefore marriage is a state proper only for heterosexuals—when the Bible is the work of man, attributed by him to God for worldly reasons. And just as man has changed his mind about some Biblically mandated prohibitions during the past two thousand years, he is likely to change his mind about gay's place in society, notwithstanding his homophobic position heretofore inscribed in Scripture and relied upon to discriminate piously against homosexuals.

An Appraisal of Rural
and Urban Life

MY GRANDFATHER ACQUIRED A HUNDRED acres in 1893, land that was hilly and rocky but forest blessed. With not much more than an axe and his wife, he hued out a space, built a house, cleared for a garden, fashioned logs into a barn, and other buildings and began to have children. My grandmother had ten children but only five boys and one girl survived. So when the boys matured their alternatives were to get another hundred acres or to go to the city to find work. My father went to the city with my mother and found work. The Roaring Twenties lured many to the cities; the Great Depression returned many to the country. I was one of them. I spent many of my happiest days on my grandfather's farm and learned to love rural ways. The sunsets viewed from the porch were exquisite poetry.

After WWII when I was in college on the GI Bill, there came a time for me to decide what to do after college. I thought seriously about going back to the farm and living the life my grandfather had. But "progress" made such a choice egregiously eccentric if not incomprehensible and economically quixotic to urban minds. So I worked a compromise: I became a teacher in winter and a farmer in summer. I am now a lawyer but I have continued to farm to some extent all my life. I believe that man and woman evolved in accordance with nature's laws and nature designed him and her to live near the land, the waters, the skies, to watch the stars and moon, to propagate, to plant and cultivate and harvest crops for their sustenance and to create artistically. I have not been alone in this strangeness of mind. Listen to Thomas Jefferson's appraisal of rural life:

"Those who labor in the earth are the chosen people of God, if ever He had a chosen people, whose breasts He has made His peculiar deposit for substantial and genuine virtue. It is the focus in which He keeps alive that sacred fire, which otherwise might escape from the face of the earth. Corruption in the morals in the mass of cultivators is a phenomenon of which no age nor nation has furnished an example. It is a mark set on those, who, not looking up to heaven, to their own soil and industry, as does the husbandman, for their sustenance, depend for it on causalities and caprice of customers.

"Dependence begets subservience and venality, suffocates the germ of virtue, and prepares fit tools for the designs of ambition. This, the natural progress and consequence of the arts, has sometimes been retarded by accidental circumstances, but, generally speaking the proportion which the aggregate of the other classes of citizens bears in any state to that of the husbandmen, is the proportion of its unsound to its healthy parts, and is a good enough barometer whereby to measure its degree of corruption." —Jefferson's "Notes on the State of Virginia."

Jefferson was a deist who considered Jesus' teachings the "most benevolent and sublime ever taught." But Jefferson did not believe that Jesus was the son of God or that he arose from the dead and is a member of the Trinity. Jefferson's God set things in motion and retired to let His infinite and omnipotent character shape the world, including life on it. And He shaped man as a part of nature just as He shaped all life evolutionarily. Thus, the virtue in man is a natural heritage, a heritage from

God. Man on the land is at home; for it is from the land he evolved. And it is the land that birthed and nourished the virtue that evolved in him, a virtue that is ever needful of closeness to its origin.

Man on the land was independent. But man in the city is dependent; and dependence "begets subservience and venality, suffocates the germ of virtue, and prepares fit tools for the designs of ambition." That is, the man who has migrated to the city and left his ax and hoe behind has "need to prepare fit tools for the designs of ambition." Jefferson wherever he is must be appalled at the multiplicities of the tools the ambitious have designed to advance their ambitions, to entice and bilk the masses in order that they may have for cheap the essential products produced by the rubes of the hinterland and have cheaply the labor of those who left the land for the sidewalks hoping to live a sweat-free life. Nature's virtue in those who design and those who suffer from the design has been undermined and compromised. Virtue hobbled the designers in their need for a life to which they were accustomed and it relegated those who were the victims of the designers to muteness faced with endless exploitation. So both, the former to exploit and the latter to fight exploitation abandoned virtue and engaged in retaliation. Virtue is a victim in the struggle between master and slave.

Corruption opines Jefferson, in a state, is greatest in the city where man is divorced from the land and less in the country where man lives on it. But the migration to cities around the world has been a 20th Century phenomenon and is continuing unabated. Mexico City now has 30 million inhabitants, all of whom left acres for streets and forests for high-rises and tenements and entered an environment fashioned by man so that he can acquire much and pay little and live from the sweat of another's brow. Divine virtue atrophies sundered from its source.

In "The Meaning of the City" Jacque Ellul supports Jefferson by enumerating the evils of the city. Here is a bit of his appraisal of urban life: "The man who disappears into the city becomes merchandise. All the inhabitants of the city are destined sooner or later to become prostitutes and members of the proletariat. And thus man's triumph, this place where he alone is king, where he sets the mark of his absolute power, where there are no traces of God's work because man has set his hand to wiping it out bit by bit, where man thinks he has found all he needs, where his situation separated from Eden becomes tolerable—this place becomes in truth the very place where he is made slave."

Crime is created; it is not innate. No person healthy of mine and body would commit a crime unless a web of circumstances, internal and external, caused him to act anti-socially. Rural environment and life conduces people to cohere communally and to eschew criminality. Whereas in the city the man-made environment, with its extremes of wealth and poverty, its void of all that is natural and appealing to the very core of man's esthetic nature, its blocks of degenerate and decadent enticements, its baited lures and conspired inducements to indulge in the fleshpots, conduces people to involve themselves in a web of circumstances that birth criminality. Jefferson's "substantial and genuine virtue," in the city, exhausts itself in search of rural nourishment and languishes for lack of it.

A Garden Veteran Returns
to One, Winter Wasted

THE GARDEN I LEARNED IN was rocky. I seldom hit a hoe lick that I didn't strike a rock. The day came when I bought some bottom land where I would have to search to find a pebble. The former garden was on a hillside and latter was flat and bounded on its northside by the Greenbrier River and on the southside by a steep hill that lay east to west. In summer the sun flooded my garden, but in winter the sun moved so far south that the hill blocked out the sun's light and warmth, sunrise to sunset, from nearly the whole of my garden. Winter has had his way with her and this winter she left a war-wasted area of bottom land.

Before that big snow in December, I went to the garden regularly to get turnips from a patch that had so many turnip leaves that I had to search for the turnips. The asparagus patch stood thick and tall. The strawberry patch was crowded with plants old and new, a green forest of them. There stood a dozen or more okra plants, some more than six feet tall. There were weedy places along the river. Even in December it was a place of life. But then came the twenty-inch snow in December, the cold and snow of January and the apocalyptic month of February. Day after day, I sat and watched the flakes fall and shoveled and swept the walks and watched them fall and shoveled and swept some more. On and on it went. The garden was out of mind.

On March the 9th the sun came out and the temperature rose to 60 degrees. I couldn't resist the invitation. I drove my truck to the garden. I hesitated at the entrance because there was still a foot of snow in the driveway and water standing in the parking area. But I decided to try it and I got over the snow and through the water to higher ground. When I got out of the truck and surveyed the garden, the word that flashed in my mind was "flattened." Nothing was standing or even kneeling or lying. Everything was flattened and covered with a gray film of dust. The thirty inches or so of snow that had come in December and January and February had weighed flat everything. The only exceptions were the turnips. Now the greens were flat but the white turnip bellies look like so many pregnancies lying on a beach.

The asparagus plants lay like a miniature forest hit with a meteor. The strawberry plants lay flat as if they had been hit by the same astronomical monster. The evidence of rhubarb required some scrutiny: it was etched in the soil. The okra plants were gone except for a splintered stump. The deer, driven to eat anything by the snow cover, had eaten the okra plants from their six-foot tops to near the surface of the garden. What was left look like an old fashioned shaving brush with its handle down in the ground and the bristles up.

The garden was a network of channels that were the work of mice seeking under the snow for some sustenance. The channels were everywhere. The sight was an Armageddon or a nuclear disaster. The only life was the pink of rhubarb emerging from a cover of death and a strawberry plant or two exhibiting the green of life. Also, even though crushed with a ton of snow, the parsley was still identifiable.

The snow and rain that came in February cause the Greenbrier River to flood. As always, the debris upriver in a flood becomes the debris downriver. And I found the gifts from upriver everywhere. One big gift was the tops of a tree that had been cut, the trunk taken, and the top left lying in what became the river bed. It was deposited on part of the garden. So I saw exercise in the warm sunshine of that day. I got axe and saw from the tool chest. And I began to do what I used to do as youth on the farm. I have converted many a tree top to a brush pile while saving whatever was suitable for the fire places.

There is a difference between 19 and 89, a difference of 70 years. But there I was doing at 89 what I had done at 19, but with a much more measured and careful pace. I had to be careful not to stumble and fall. So with deliberation and calculation, I picked up my axe and waded into the thicket of a tree top. I selected out the obvious limbs and pulled them from the mass and tossed them where I planned to pile what was brush and to save what was firewood. Then I took my axe and began to cut the small limbs from the larger limbs. I piled the smaller stuff and I cut the larger limbs into lengths I could handle and deposited them for future hauling to the house. My accuracy with an axe had deteriorated since I was 19 but it was accurate enough to cut away the larger limbs and to finally succeed in having a brush pile and some wood for the stove.

I then turned my attention to my blackberry patch. It had withstood the snow onslaught but was in need of having last year's dead canes cut and removed and this year's canes tied to metal posts for support. In my tool chest I had pruning shears to cut the old canes and other extraneous growth that competed with blackberry canes. I worked methodically from one patch to another, cutting out the old canes and tying up the new. After a while the blackberry patch was cleaned of the extraneous and was set for the season and the production of gallons of berries.

I was tiring. I hadn't had so much exercise in months. I decided to try to pull up the okra stumps as a last chore. I had trouble with many of them. I couldn't pull them out. I did succeed in pulling out a number of them and I tossed them on the compost pile.

I took a few minutes to look at the garden and the condition it was in after I had spent the afternoon trying to rescue it from winter's devastation. I felt a physical gladness and relief and an esthetic joy. I had begun another year of gardening. I would have, if all goes well, another chance to dance with nature, to plant seeds, cultivate them and nurture them. And realize the goals of such works: to be able to table the foodstuffs that sustain life, to be able to do physical work in the open and under sky and sun, and to be able to feel the blessedness of rest after work's fatigue.

Secular Mann

The Infamous Homicide

ON FEBRUARY 17, 1600, PURSUANT to a decree of inquisitional authorities, executioners brought a philosopher-priest from a dungeon where he had languished for seven years, stripped him of his clothing, gagged him, and in the center of Rome's Campo di Fiori square burned him to death. His crime was that he had contumaciously over a period of ten years refused to recant his belief, among others, that the earth was not the center of the universe and not the body around which the sun revolved.

The Church considered this man's ideas so dangerous his publications were placed on the Index, a list of publications that were forbidden by the Church for the eyes of the faithful; and his works were destroyed when they came into the hands of authorities, leaving few for posterity. He died anathematized and friendless. But his ideas could not be destroyed; and in spite of the Church's effort to eradicate them, they took root in the 19th century and flourished. The philosopher-priest was rediscovered and honored 299 years later on the very date he was executed and in the very spot by the erection of a monument to him.

Yearly since on the anniversary of his execution, admirers from many countries have come to the square to honor the secular martyr, the scientific saint, who read Copernicus and not only believed him but incorporated his astronomical findings into a new philosophy and new concept of God. And on the four hundredth anniversary, February 17, 2000, admiring freethinkers came again to praise the man, and the radicals came to damn the Church. One sign at the base of his statue read: "He was killed because he thought freely" and denounced the "infamous homicide."

A Vatican spokesman called the execution on February 17, 1600, of the Renaissance heretic Giordano Bruno "a sad episode of modern Christian history." The Church has declined to go so far in the case of Bruno as it did in 1992 in the case of Galileo, who committed the same sin, by overruling the Inquisition and declaring the conviction of Galileo the result of a "tragic mutual incomprehension."

Other than believing what no one in any church on the planet would deny today, what did Giordano Bruno believe and write that provoked the Inquisition to order such a final solution in his case? First, Bruno did not believe God sat on a throne in Heaven above and perpendicular to Jerusalem and the devil ruled in Hell located beneath the city with angels and devils coming and going to intervene in human affairs, while God kept books on everyone and looked down on a fixed planet that He had created in a week's work. But he believed that the earth revolved around the sun, that the sun was a star similar to an infinite number of other stars with planets, that natural laws and processes were the same everywhere in the universe, and that God was not apart from earth or the universe but was in fact a part and the whole of everything, including all that was organic or inorganic. God was here and everywhere, not somewhere out there.

He was a pantheist; that is, he believed that God was present throughout nature and was one and the same as nature and that nature including man reflected His characteristics. Pantheism was Bruno's belief that the Holy Inquisition could not countenance and allow to be spread; for it was antithetical to the

Church's basic theological premise that God was separate from nature; that He had appeared among men incarnate, etc., etc.

Further, Bruno departed from the Church in other matters. He taught man's chief concern should be the expulsion from his nature the beast and the triumph of truth and other virtues in his character and conduct and moral progress was an unending struggle in the direction of an infinite goal, advancement toward which was happiness. He apparently did not believe that imitation of Christ was impossible and that man must rely on the grace of God and the intermediation of the Church for salvation.

Giordano knew little of peace or prosperity in his life. He went into a monastery at age 14, and owing to his independent thinking, he was charged with entertaining heretical ideas and fled the sanctuary. He went from country to country over a period of 16 years trying in vain to find a place of refuge where he could live, study, teach, and write undisturbed. At times he experienced extreme poverty, and at other times he received recognition and taught in some of the great universities. His prosperity whenever it came was short lived, for he could not be tolerated by Christians believing as he did that the earth moves around the sun and his inferences therefrom.

His admirers at the 400th anniversary tribute acted, one observer noted, as if he had been murdered just yesterday instead of four hundreds years ago. It is not difficult to understand why they acted so. The same inquisitional mindset is afoot today and would incite the persecution of heretics save that it is without the devices, at least in the West, of ecclesiastical police and courts and the power of torture and execution.

There are those who would burn books that teach evolution; who believe their brand of religion is so true they feel compelled to proselytize people of, to them, inferior faiths; and who believe and teach a theology as primitive as the one current in the days of Giordano. And there are those who look upon the wall separating church and state as a devil's design to make easier the corruption of youth and would breach it had they the power.

Giordano's only crime was that he thought differently and freely and rationally, accepting and teaching at his peril what is now accepted universally as truth. Surely, such an injustice caused angels to cry and should have taught humankind not only appearances are often misleading but also dogmatism arising from appearances is a sandy premise upon which to plan or build anything, much less a premise upon which to burn to death a good, learned, and courageous free thinker with the courage to speak as he thought.

Jefferson helped make America safe for free thinkers by building the wall. Giordano somewhere may take comfort from and have his hopes resurrected by what Jefferson did and American courts have reaffirmed. So far.

Conspicuous Discrepancies
in the New Testament

"THE BIBLE IS SO HUMAN a book that I don't see how belief in its divine authorship can survive the reading of it." William James, in response to a 1904 survey of religious belief.

"The problem is in part that the Gospels are full of discrepancies and were written decades after Jesus's ministry and death by authors who had not themselves witnessed any of the events." Bart D. Ehrman in his book "Jesus Interrupted."

I have recently finished reading Ehrman's book. He confirms with solid scholarship my agnostic suspicions that the New Testament is, among many proffered books, a selection of them written by men and chosen by like-thinking theologians, that the original works are gone and the books are all copies, that it is the child of oral transmissions over decades, that each Gospel presents a different Jesus, that the miracles are myths, that the Resurrection is hearsay, that the Apocalypse is fanciful imagining and that the Trinity is an evolved and man-made concept.

It is interesting that Ehrman, prior to entering a seminary, was a fundamentalist Christian who believed in the inerrancy of the Bible. But what he learned at the seminary induced him to become an agnostic. He writes that what he learned at the seminary has been taught there for decades to aspiring preachers, and he wonders why most congregations are ignorant of what is taught in the seminaries. Of course, the answer is that the churches do not want people to know that truth for obvious reasons. The Catholic Church opposed vehemently the translation of the Bible into the vernacular of the countries of Europe.

Ehrman: "Jesus' teaching in Mark is apocalyptic: 'This time has been fulfilled' implies that this current evil age, seen on a time line, is almost over. The end is in sight. 'The Kingdom of God is near' means that God will soon intervene in this age and overthrow its wicked powers and the kingdoms they support, such as Rome, and establish his own kingdom, a kingdom of truth, peace, and justice."

Mark's Jesus believes the kingdom is soon to come: "Truly I tell you, some of those standing here will not taste death before they see the Kingdom of God having come to power." In Mark, Jesus never refers to himself as a divine being, as someone who preexisted, as someone who was in any sense equal with God. In Mark, he is not God and he does not claim to be.

But by the time John wrote his Gospel "those standing" were all gone, and the Kingdom had not come, so John presents a different Jesus, one who is not an apocalypticist teaching that the end is near but one claiming to be God and the way to salvation and eternal life.

Ehrman: "Things are quiet different in the Gospel of John. In Mark, Jesus teaches principally about God and the coming of the kingdom, hardly ever about himself, except to say that he must go to Jerusalem to be executed, whereas in John, that is practically all that Jesus talks about: who he is, where he has come from, where he is going, and how he is the one who can provide eternal life."

As to Jesus' miracles, Ehrman makes this point: "Whereas supernatural proofs of Jesus' identity were strictly off limits in Matthew, in John they are the principal reason for Jesus' miraculous acts."

St. Paul and Matthew's Jesus differ irreconcilably on whether or not the keeping of Jewish law was a requisite to salvation. Matthew's Jesus declared keeping them was necessary to know salvation. Paul was of the opinion that it was not necessary. Salvation to him was a matter of faith in Jesus and in his death and resurrection.

Why did Jesus die? Mark is clear that Jesus' death brought about an atonement for sin. Mark's Jesus: "The Son of Man came not to be served but to serve, and to give his life as a ransom for many." That is, Jesus died to ransom others from the debt they owed to God because of their sins. The death is an atonement.

Luke, to the contrary, deleted the atonement reason for Jesus's death and replaced it with his view: Salvation comes not through an atoning sacrifice but by forgiveness that comes with repentance. In Mark, Jesus died to pay for the sins of men. In Luke Jesus died to forgive the debt.

In the Fourth century, after Constantine had a vision of Christ and believed that he helped him to win a critical battle, he became a Christian. But to disturb the peace of the empire came Arianism, the belief that God and Jesus were not of the same substance since there was the Father then came the son. Thus, the son had to be subordinate to the Father. This controversy was so threatening that Constantine convened a council of Bishops at Nicaea in 325 CE to decide whether God and Jesus were of the same substance or not. The Emperor got what he wanted: the bishops voted that the Father and the son were of the same substance. Then there were two of the Trinity, which was to evolve, fathered by the bishops, in which the Godhead consists of the Father, the Son and the Holy Ghost, each one equally God, eternal and of the same substance. Figure that.

I agree with Williams James's observation that the Bible is so human a book its divine authorship cannot survive the reading of it. The God of the Hebrew Testament was cruel, vengeful, and autocratic. He had all the failings associated with humans in extreme.

Jesus is closer to being a divine being owing to his biographers' efforts to create a divine and supernatural being. That decades past between Jesus' crucifixion and the writings of the Gospels and that even the synoptic Gospels contain conspicuous discrepancies cause one to question their divine nature. John obviously was of a mind to make Jesus God even though his Gospel was written 85 years after the fact. The Christian churches have built upon the creed instead of the Sermon. They have built upon sand as time will tell.

Mischief Birthed by Believers of the Bible's Inerrancy

THE JUDAIC PRIESTHOOD PUT CHRIST on the cross notwithstanding that Pontius Pilate found Christ's kingdom no threat to Roman rule. The reigning religious hierarchy, the Pharisees and Scribes, judged Jesus's teachings blasphemous and subversive. They could suffer the blasphemy, but they could not abide Jesus's threat to their ecclesiastical hegemony, their perks and power, and the challenge to their laws, laws they proclaimed to be promulgated by God and transmitted to Moses on a stage set on Sinai.

Christ's alleged resurrection gave rise to Christendom, which added to the Hebrew Bible the Gospels, Acts, St. Paul, and Revelations. Martin Luther's introspection convinced him that good works and the mass could not, but that faith and grace could, get him to heaven. Thus, came the Reformation and with it a modification of interpretation of the Scriptures and God's words. And also followed sectarian wars whose perpetrators reduced to ruins by arson, pillage, rape, and slaughter much of Europe.

Subsequently, Protestants splintered into hundreds of sects, each proclaiming that its reading and interpretations of the Bible to be in exact accordance with the spirit and letter of the words of God and His Son, thus, each sect asserting one book was God's revealed truth, and, therefore, no one need seek any further than the Bible for the Truth. And each taught his children so, and his children taught his children so for generations. And this generation is no different.

In Missouri, Senator John Ashcroft, a Republican of the Christian right, was in a battle with Democratic Gov. Carnahan for a seat in the U.S. Senate. The Wall Street Journal in a take on the race sized up Ashcroft: "There is a rock-hard certainty about him, a conviction that most issues come down to a simple right or wrong – and that he knows which is which."

As Ashcroft put it in a book he wrote about his preacher father: "Many people paralyze themselves trying to figure out the will of God, but Dad taught that where God's will is clearly laid out in Scripture, we do not have to figure it out; we just have to do it."

Ashcroft was an anti-abortionist, an ally of the NRA, an advocate of the death penalty, and had an honorary degree from Bob Jones University, whose president believed the Catholic Church is the Anti-Christ, and blacks and whites should not mix maritally, all of which political postures Ashcroft no doubt believed to be God's will. Because his daddy told him so.

I would guess that Ashcroft believed in Creation as opposed to evolution, in prayer in schools, in the capitalistic system, in the Trinity, the Resurrection, Biblical Miracles, etc., and believed that socialists, environmentalists and homosexuals are abominations in the eyes of God. All of which truths he believed because they are in the Bible, and thus are God's will. And because his daddy said they are so.

The more conservative Baptists have recently met and have decided that only males are fit to be pastors and they have founded the decision on Scripture, specifically, the words of St. Paul, whose words they consider God's words just as they consider every word in the Bible to be His word, and further just as they believe that every word of which is to be taken literally, even the myth that God put all this together in six days way back some few thousands years ago.

It is passing strange, and it is the mother of all paradoxes that a religion that is called Christian is absent Christ, he who Christians believe was God. Nietzsche a century ago observed Jesus was the last Christian. He had ample evidence to conclude he was, and were Nietzsche alive today he would have no reason to conclude otherwise. The Christian right of which Ashcroft is member is a misnomer. It is right, all right; but it is not Christian.

Anyone who reads the Sermon on the Mount and compares the moral concepts therein with Ashcroft's interpretations of God's will and the Christian right's concepts will note a canyon of contradictions. In fact, there is little in American politics and in its religious principles that are compatible with the teachings of Jesus. Ashcroft, or anyone else, would have long been on a cross had he preached and lived the teachings and life of Christ.

The premise the Bible is the word of God and manifests God's will is palpably vulnerable to contradiction, not necessarily upon the ground of scholarly studies but simply upon the ground of common sense and imagination. A close reading of the Bible, particularly of the Old Testament, reveals man's hand and mind everywhere, as evidenced by his biases and prejudices, his hopes and dreams, and his inferences and speculations writ therein.

Since Christians believe that God came to earth as Jesus in order to teach man His will face to face, how do they reconcile their insistence on prayer at football games with God's Son's exhortation that they pray in secret in their closets; or reconcile their thirst for vengeance in the death penalty with Jesus's teaching that they should do good for evil, turn the other cheek, and forgive not once but seven times seventy; or their cheers for welfare reform with Jesus' reminder that to do unto the least is to do unto him; or their hard-rock certainty with his admonition that the meek shall inherit the earth?

Is God's will to be found in the Old Testament or in the Gospels? Certainly, His will cannot be in both; for the former is morally primitive relative to the latter. An eye-for-an-eye is in the opposite moral pole from turn-the-other-cheek; thou shall not kill is easy morality compared with Christ's word that one is in danger of damnation if he is so much as angry with his fellow man; for one to abstain from adultery is no big problem relative to not even lusting after a woman in one's mind. And the omission by the Pharisees of tending to the wounds and needs of an ethnically undesirable, measured by the empathic commission of the Good Samaritan, emphasizes graphically the moral gulf between Leviticus and Luke's Gospel.

To teach a child God revealed truth to man and the revelation is all bound in the Bible does an indelible disservice to a child because it has a tendency to make of him a person with a hard-rock certainty, an arrogant person, and a person intolerant of any other person's perception of truth. To wit: John Ashcroft.

Further, it fosters fanaticism. Anti-abortionists are so certain of what is God's will that some of them wait in hiding and shoot doctors in the back to the cheers of other anti-abortionists, all believing that God cheers with them.

Also, accepting the Bible as Truth, and literally, causes one to react defensively, even violently, when his belief is seriously challenged. Fear enters his heart and mind when the premises of his thinking and acting are shaken because he has no philosophical flexibility or stability on which to rely resulting from an independent investigation of the meaning of life and way to live it.

There is no hard proof that the Bible is God's word or reflects God's will, even though some of it God might agree with. What is more likely is that man cites man when he cites Scripture but attributes it to God to give it the authority of the Omniscient.

History tells the tale of the consequences of teaching that one book contains all Truth and that the book is the dictates of God to man. It is a tale of men so hard-rock certain of their beliefs they tortured and murdered many whose only sin was to think independently and differently. To wit: Christ's crucifixion and The Inquisition.

I submit that it is better that one paralyze himself trying to figure out God's will rather than accept unquestionably that His will is revealed in a single book and upon that belief work zealously to impose one's interpretation of it upon his children and everyone else.

Further, one of the most exciting and rewarding voyages of life, for anyone, is to leave home's haven, to sail the seas of doubt and exploration, and to return with a cargo of humble confidence in the understanding of what the good life is.

Jefferson Contradicts the Claim of the Christians

IF ONE HAS BEEN COGNIZANT of religious matters for the past twenty years, he is aware that Christian Fundamentalists consider this nation to be a Christian Nation. As evidence they often offer the religious beliefs of the Founding Fathers. In doing so they are ignorant of the beliefs of Benjamin Franklin, John Adams, James Madison, Thomas Paine, and particularly Thomas Jefferson.

Jefferson wrote: "I am a Christian, in the only sense he wished any one to be; sincerely attached to his doctrines, in preference to all others; ascribing to himself every human excellence; and believing he never claimed any other." That is, Jesus was a man of the greatest human excellences, but he was not the son of a God, nor did he die, resurrect and ascend to heaven to sit at the right hand of his Father. Jefferson was not a Trinitarian or believer in the Nicene Creed.

In a letter to Samuel Kercheval, dated January 19, 1810, in response to a letter received from him regarding the corrupting of Jesus's teachings, Jefferson wrote this in his reply: "… that but a short time elapsed after the death of the great reformer of the Jewish religion, before his principles were departed from by those who professed to be his special servants, and perverted into an engine for enslaving mankind, and aggrandizing their oppressors in Church and State: that the purest system of morals ever before preached to man has been adulterated and sophisticated by artificial constructions, into a mere contrivance to filch wealth and power to themselves: that rational men, not being able to swallow their impious heresies, in order to force them down their throats, they raise the hue and cry of infidelity, while themselves are the greatest obstacles to the advancement of the real doctrines of Jesus, and do, in fact, constitute the real Anti-Christ."

If Jefferson scanned the channels of today's TV offerings and came upon the revolting and shocking spectacle of thousand-dollar suited evangelists presiding at the contrived and fraudulent miraculous healing of the sick, sore, lame, and disabled by the laying on of their hands; and had he knowledge of the income of such impious impostures claiming apostolic succession from the humble Carpenter of Galilee, he would take note that not much has changed, since his day, in the world of Orthodox Christianity.

In his book "The God Delusion" Richards Dawkins quotes Jefferson often and one of his favorite quotes is from a letter written by Jefferson to Peter Carr from Paris, August 10, 1787: "Shake off all the fears of servile prejudices, under which weak minds are servilely crouched. Fix reason firmly in her seat, and call to her tribunal every fact, every opinion. Question with boldness even the existence of a God: because, if there is one, he must more approve of the homage of reason than that of blind-folded fear."

Jefferson read the Gospels and found much in them not compatible with the intrinsic nature of Jesus and discovered a multitude of myths that had been forever associated with prophets, and he decided he would write his own Bible leaving out the political and theological interpolations and the miracles, all of which he considered alien to Jesus's teachings and character, but all essential to the establishment, in Jesus's name, of a worldly religious organization designed to perpetuate and support an ecclesiastical hierarchy and church.

In a letter to Francis Adrian van der Kemp, a Dutch scholar and Unitarian minister, Jefferson outlined his project to restore to the Gospels their original purity and to excise those Scriptures he believed were incompatible with Jesus' words and acts: "Among the sayings and discourses imputed to Him by His biographers, I find many passages of fine imagination, correct morality, and of the most lovely benevolence; and others, again, of so much ignorance, so much absurdity, so much untruth, charlatanism and imposture, as to pronounce it impossible that such contradictions should have proceeded from the same Being. I separate, therefore, the gold from the dross; restore to Him the former, and leave the latter to the stupidity of some, and roguery of others of His disciples."

The result of his project was the "The Jefferson Bible," a remarkable achievement in which he surveyed the four gospels and excised those Scriptures he considered to be the interpolations and opportunistic additions of worldly clerics and were, in Jefferson judgment, words and concepts Jesus would never have uttered and miracles he never performed.

One reads in Mark 16: 15-18: "And he said unto them, 'Go ye into the world, and preach the gospel to every creature. He that believeth and is baptized shall be saved; but he that believeth not shall be damned. And these signs shall follow them that believe; In my name shall they cast out devils; they shall speak with new tongues; They shall take up serpents; and if they drink any deadly thing, it shall not hurt them; they shall lay hands on the sick, and they shall recover.'"

Jefferson excised those verses from his Gospel of Mark. Anyone who thinks and studies and perceives the true Jesus would not only excise those scriptures but would wonder how they ever became a part of Mark or any other of the Gospels, except that they were appended to the end of Mark's Gospel to give credence to the belief that Jesus was God. Yet from these specious sayings there have arisen a number of sects and denominations with large followings.

The Pentecostals, a member of which is a former Attorney-General of the United States, believe in "new tongues," or glossolalia. There are preachers who, wherever they can pitch a tent or afford a TV station, will induce and seduce the gullible to come to sit entranced as the lame throw away their crutches and the blind see again. Further, there has arisen from the verses the belief that, in order to be saved and live a postmortem life in Paradise, one must be baptized and profess a belief in Christ. It strains credulity to believe that Jesus would countenance the sending of a life-long scoundrel to heaven who believed and had been baptized and send a saint to hell who had not believed and been baptized. Then there are some who handle snakes but there are few who drink deadly things to test their faith.

Lastly, Jefferson's Bible concludes Matthews' Gospel thusly: "And rolled a great stone to the door of sepulcher, and departed." That is not only the end of Jefferson's Matthews but the end of his Mark, Luke, and John. There is nothing about Jesus' Resurrection, Reappearance, or Ascension in the Jefferson Bible. Jefferson views the teachings of Jesus as lovely benevolences, but he did not believe the miracles and the incompatible and incredible interpolations attributed to him. Thus, Jefferson was not a Christian, notwithstanding the Christians' contention.

Fourscore is Enough

EVERY BIRTH IS NO LESS than twins: life and death. As soon as there is birth, death stalks the new life. Nature designed it that way. What nature had in mind is biological balance. It is obvious if life had not included death as a twin and if everything that had received life were still around, life would be piled upon life, every species of which would be gasping and grasping for earth and air and whatever else needed for it to continue. Life would be a living death rather than a life and a death.

A world without death would be the creation of some omnipotent sentimentalist, the kind that places pictures and mawkish poetry in papers on Memorial Day, or of some wizard holed up in a lab with the genome reduced to a keyboard by which he arranges the genes and introduces cellular cement at critical places to regenerate where atrophy has set in, giving men and women the opportunity to endure the same quotidian quandary and live through the same drama of bliss and agony for two hundred years plus, instead of Jehovah's bequest of threescore and ten.

The advocates of working toward life everlasting on earth with a Wal-Mart and a McDonald's at hand have met with resistance. One ethicist appalled by the prospect speaks bluntly: "We can't ban this research but we can make it socially despicable." One backing mother nature says: "The finitude of human life is a blessing for every individual whether he knows it or not." And another argues that the natural ambitions of family and career can be satisfied within a life span of 80 years. Amen.

A theologian of Christian persuasion opposes lengthening life on the ground that doing so delays the day of the faithful's union with God. A Rabbi, on the other hand, without belief in a hereafter and with an eye on this world, believes everything that can be done should be done to prolong life.

A Catholic theologian is irate: He criticizes the search for immortality as a "pagan and sub-Christian quest and an enterprise driven by the essentially amoral and mindless dynamic of the technological imperative joined to an ignoble fear of death." His excessive protest manifests a concern that scientists will usurp the need for salvation, the unique employment of ecclesiastics.

Now into my 93rd year, I have, by virtue of having lived so long, the credentials to speak on this issue. Up front I admit to being a pagan, a secular humanist in moderation, an immoderate Luddite, and a reasonable romantic. Each facet of my being reacts to the prospects of extended life differently. As a pagan I reluctantly agree with the Catholic, even though he seems to take a dim view of pagans and sub-Christians, whatever they are. I agree that it is revolting and disgusting to read about Frankensteins in workshops delving into the mysteries of nature with a view to clone species and to prolong life by all manner of weird, strange, and unnatural manipulations, transplants, organ-production, and by works heretofore considered only by the minds of latter-day alchemists and madmen with knowledge supplied by the Devil or by those who have sold their souls to Mephistopheles.

I hasten to say, lest some pagan god trip me up for apostasy, I do not, as the Christians do, oppose longer life because it delays union with God. I do not believe that life after death is any more than a return of my substance to the earth to fertilize other life. My consciousness, declared an eternal soul by robed intermediaries interested in my allegiance in exchange for assistance in transferring it from this world to the next, is no more, I suspect, than an electromagnetic field that collapses when death shuts off the life current that flows in my being.

The Catholic is irate owing to the challenge of the technological imperative to the raison d'etre of the church: that is, the administering of sacraments that are prerequisites to salvation. With indefinite life and no fear of death who is interested in an institution that sells life hereafter?

I have preached that, if the church were to say that its only mission is to teach Jesus' moral challenge and help mankind to live it and not to assure people that through its rituals and intercession life eternal is a certainty, the priests and preachers would surely be heard only by the choir and a reduced choir at that.

Jews do not believe in an after life, so I can understand why a Rabbi would advocate prolonging life by every means possible. To some extent I can understand his view but not entirely. I flinch emotionally, some aspect of my being recoils, when I read about scientists using stem cells to reproduce organs that are to be used to replace worn out organs. There is something about such a procedure that is blatant violation of the laws of nature. But violating or attempting to violate the laws of nature has been man's preoccupation ever since he was evicted from Eden.

Nature made man to work. He found, though, that work of a physical kind is an inconvenience and discomfort to him, so he has put lesser folks or machines to work and used his leisure to pleasure himself, the consequence of which has been the deterioration of his heart and other organs. But rather than give up the leisure, he devised means to replace the abused heart; he plans to replace, if he can conquer the obstacles, every organ that sputters and conks out in man's engine with no regard to how profligate and ruinous has been his lifestyle. One can forgive another seven times seventy; but when it comes to footing the bill for multiple transplants for an incorrigible hedonist, there has to be an end. Death quiets the blood.

I am a Luddite. I lived when a man learned to work with a hoe and a scythe rather to play with a golf club and a tennis racket. I have watched the escalation of technology with at first excitement and then concern and now scorn and contempt. What is the end of all this? What if man comes to know all truth, to be able to transport himself to any place in a flash, to communicate with anyone at any time, to do anything or all things, to have all joys with no sorrows, and to live however long he wills? What then? The sensible will tend a garden and await the end, working humbly amid the mysteries of creation.

As a romantic I think of A. E. Housman's lament: "And since to look at things in bloom / Fifty springs are little room, About the woodland I will go / To see the cherry hung with snow." And I think how true, having now even less left than little room. So I might consider a reprieve from death indefinitely for room to go about the woodland in spring and see the cherry blooming and wearing white for Eastertide.

Criticizing Religious Irrationality

"THERE IS, IN FACT, NOT much to secularism that should be of interest to anyone, apart from the fact that it is all that stands between sensible people like ourselves and the mad hordes of religious imbeciles who have balkanized our world, impeded the progress of science, and now place civilization itself in jeopardy. Criticizing religious irrationality is absolutely essential." Sam Harris, Rational Mysticism, published in Free Enquiry.

The quote by Sam Harris is out of context just as every quote is. But except for his view that "there is a kernel of truth in the grandiosity and otherworldly language of religion," and the following passage: "Faith enables many of us to endure life's difficulties with an equanimity that would be scarcely conceivable in a world lit only by reason," he bends little from affirming the view expressed in his quote at the beginning of this article.

Imbecile is a harsh word to hurl at anyone, but what can one say when reason is applied to those Muslim fanatics in Palestine and Iraq who drop on their knees and bend to Mecca five times a day and between prayers help harness fellow Muslims with explosives that slaughter the intended enemies and often kill innocents and babes in arms. The motive is a combination of tribalism, religion, and despair. They die for their country and their God with the dream for their sacrifice they will be lifted from despair to a heaven of pleasures forever. For the realization of this dream, conjured and preached by mullahs, the "imbeciles" gladly blow themselves to bits and many others to bits as a result of the irrationality that has been preached to them.

The Jews believe that God chose them especially in preference to all other peoples, and in confirmation of that choice He conveyed to them in perpetuity the Holy Land. Why God allowed other tribes to conquer and disperse the Jews throughout the world is a mystery that is explained somewhat, however, by the prophets as punishment for their sins. But now they are back in the Holy Land, having displaced Palestinians by arms and still are declaring that they are there legitimately on the ground that God gave them the land for theirs to have and to hold forever.

What does reason say to the assertion that God gave land to any tribe or to anyone else in perpetuity? The Indians of North America might make the same claim to the United States with as much legitimacy as the Jews do to the Holy Land, if one reads the Indians' bible. The answer to such a claim is the claimant is an imbecile, or at least his reason is so atrophied by religion and faith he cannot think rationally. Nationalism and religion seem to do to reason what sexual infatuation does to common sense—but often with worse consequences.

The Popes have long proclaimed with regard to morality and other matters their proclamations and pontifications are infallible. Who but one made imbecilic by indoctrination from childhood would accept such a belief? An infallible Pope once told his flock Earth was the center of the Universe. An infallible Pope once told his flock God created the earth, the heavens, night and day, seasons, grass and trees, man and women and the whole of everything inhabiting earth in a period of six days.

An infallible Pope now sides with Darwin with the exception that somewhere in the evolutionary chain of life humankind was given a soul that is eternal. And to realize an eternity in bliss one must do as the Pope instructs through his agents.

And then there are the Baptist and Evangelical fundamentalists. They believe in the inerrancy of the Bible; that is, they believe every word of it is the word of God revealed to Moses, Christ, St Paul, and other prophets. How any rational person can read the Bible from beginning to end, read Leviticus and all the other books of the Hebrew Bible in which Jehovah conspires with the Jews to exterminate thousands of their enemies and rejoices in the sack and plunder; and then read the Gospels and Jesus's Sermon on the Mount—and still maintain that every word of the Bible is God's word—is a mystery explained only by the atrophy of his reason. The God of the Hebrew Bible has little in common with the Father of Christ. Jehovah would have an adulteress stoned to death, a horrible death even to contemplate. Christ's sentence of the woman caught in adultery was "Go and sin no more."

The fundamentalists believe, believe it or not, that the Holy Ghost fathered Jesus immaculately and Mary, to her surprise, conceived and birthed him. They believe that Jesus walked on water, raised the dead to life, died on the cross, rose from his sepulcher, ascended to Heaven, and now sits at the right hand of God Almighty. And he did all this for the sake of all of us to redeem our sins. They also believe in heaven and hell, and they believe for one to get to heaven, one must experience full immersion baptism, believe that salvation is dependent upon faith alone, and accept Jesus Christ as savior. And they believe all those who do not abide by all of this nonsense will go to hell. No god in his right mind would ever agree with and confirm such irrationality. Clerics through the ages have either dreamed this theology and believed it or have schemed it in order to gain power over the masses.

The people nearly had to contend with the decisions of Harriet Miers, whom George Bush nominated a justice of the Supreme Court to replace Sandra O'Conner but who was not confirmed. Ms. Miers was a member of the Valley View Christian Church of Dallas, which on its Web site revealed "it believes in Biblical inerrancy, full immersion baptism, original sin, and salvation dependent entirely upon accepting Jesus Christ."

How, in this world of libraries in every town and village and computers now in every household and in schools and offices—can one still believe in the irrationality subscribed to by the church Ms. Miers attended? Particularly, how could Harriet Miers, who earned a college and law degree and had had all the advantages of a well-off person as well as never having had her time consumed by a family or even a husband—not expanded her mind beyond Fundamentalist theology? It's a mystery to me and a depressing revelation. If Miers had been confirmed and voted with John Roberts to overturn Roe v. Wade, in a world crowded with the animal Homo sapiens, there would have been abortions in the alleys and duped and seduced women made criminals. Religionists are helping to create a world that would appall Christ.

Sun Worship

EARLIEST MAN WORSHIPPED THE SUN. The sun was his god; for he knew without the sun he was done. Modern man takes the sun for granted. He even knows an eclipse of the sun is temporary. But if he thinks on the subject, he admits to himself without the sun he too is done and all else is gone. The earth was a goddess, for man knew that if she did not provide a bountiful harvest, he would be reduced to beggary and failing that starvation. So he prayed to earth goddesses and sacrificed to them with faith they would arrange for him to have rain, sun, and warmth to resurrect seeds to provide the grain for his table.

Man still, in a pagan manner, worships the sun and the earth but it is a worship that is superimposed by Christian rituals. The Winter Solstice to the Pagans was a time of concern that the sun's daily diminution would continue, but when it became apparent a few days after the Solstice the sun was returning, it was a time of great rejoicing and celebration. The Christian fathers decided rightly that it was politic to join the Pagans rather than offend those it wanted to convert, so the Winter Solstice is the birthday of Christ. And thus the holly, fir, and red ribbons are as much a part of Christmas as are the creche, cross, and Three Wise Men.

Easter is a Pagan holiday that also has a superimposition: that of the Christian celebration of the Resurrection, another political move of the church to win over Pagans. Spring is when Pagans rejoiced, thanked their gods for the vernal equinox and that time when the birds returned, the buds bloomed, the grass grew green, and every living thing awoke and stirred and regenerated itself in some manner, all to the good of man and all life. Christ rose, but so did everything else the Sunday after the full moon after the equinox.

The Christians, once Constantine established their church as the state's church, began to give the Pagans a hard time. It was an eye for an eye instead of the other cheek. According to Gilbert Murray in his book "Five Stages of Greek Religion," the Christians pinned their faith to the approaching end of the world by fire. "They announced the end of the world as near, and they rejoiced in the prospect of its destruction....It was widely believed that Christian fanatics had from time to time actually tried to light fires which would consume the accursed world and thus hasten the coming of the kingdom which should bring incalculable rewards to their own organization and plunge the rest of mankind in everlasting torment."

Thus, it seems Christians then had more interest in the next world than they did in this world and looked to the church more for salvation than instruction in Christian ethics. The church was looked upon then as now as a vehicle to ride to heaven instead of an oracle to hear how to live.

"John 3:16" is seen along every highway and on ever religious pamphlet. But one never reads any where except in his Bible: "Turn the other cheek." The promise of Salvation supercedes exhortation to do good for wrong and other ethical exhortations in the Sermon on the Mount.

If it were ethics Christians felt a need for, they had only to search Pagan literature, and they would have found essentially what Christ taught. But they were looking for a Heaven hereafter. In his book Murray quotes a Pagan prayer attributed to

"Eusebius, a late Iconic Platonist of whom almost nothing is known, not even the date which he lived: "May I be no man's enemy, and may I be the friend of that which is eternal and abides. May I never quarrel with those nearest to me, and if I do, may I be reconciled quickly. May I never devise evil against any man; if any devise evil against me, may I escape uninjured and without need of hurting him. May I seek love, seek, and attain only that which is good. May I wish for all men's happiness and envy none. May I never rejoice in the ill-fortune of one who has wronged me….When I have done what is wrong, may I never wait for the rebuke of others, but always rebuke myself until I make amends….May I win no victory that harms either me or my opponent….May I reconcile friends who are wroth with one another. May I, to the extent of my power, give all needful help to my friends and to all who are in want. May I never fail a friend in danger. When visiting those in grief may I be able by gentle and healing words to soften their pain….May I respect myself….May I always keep tame that which rages within me….May I accustom myself to be gentle, and never be angry with people because of circumstances. May I never discuss who is wicked and what wicked things he has done, but know good men and follow in their footsteps."

Christ would have said amen to Eusebius's prayer. He would have because there is much in it that Christ preached: "Therefore, if thou bring a gift to the altar, and there rememberest that thy brother hath ought against thee;… first be reconciled to thy brother, and then come and offer thy gift."

Saint Paul also would have found compatible concepts: He said that charity suffers long and is kind, and it does not envy others or rejoice in iniquity.

There are other Pagans who voiced their hearts and minds in a manner similar to Eusebius and who even surpassed him in moral eloquence and rational ethics. Christ was not born in a moral atmosphere that was totally Judaic. The Greeks and the Romans had left their moral imprint before Christ came. Thus, the Pagans built a religious and ethical foundation upon which Christianity decided to build in view of its deep-rootedness in the culture of man. That ethics of all religions are similar should engender religious toleration, even of Paganism.

The Return of the Sun

WHATEVER MADE THE UNIVERSE KNEW its geometry. It knew that if it tilted the earth's axis 23.5 degrees from the perpendicular of the plane of the earth's orbit around the sun, there would be seasons on that tilted planet, a blessing whose worth it reckoned would be beyond calculation.

In the northern climes, at this time of the year of the earth's orbit, all life, whether or not it has knowledge of geometry, rejoices in the return of the sun and the start—but also the beginning of the end—of winter. For all life instinctively, if not consciously, is aware that without the sun, not even shriven hope would know salvation.

In cities and suburbs where lights hold back darkness and obscure the heavens and where thermostats activate central heating when temperature drops below a degree that maintains cozy comfort, the sun is taken for granted and is given little notice. That the sun is the source of life for everything, that it grows the food for all life, warms the earth, gives inspiration by its dawn and twilights and its rising and settings to the eyes and souls of peasants and patricians, the dumb and the smart, the illiterate and the artist—is little noticed by cosmopolites relative to how the sun was noted by primitive peoples.

One can imagine how it was once man had gained consciousness of a past, present, and future and yet knew nothing of the heavens and their workings. One can imagine that in the north, he was getting uneasy by the end of October, for he noticed that day after day the sun was with him a shorter time, and its rays when it was with him were not so warming. Suppose, he worried, its presence continues slowly to decrease and its warmth to attenuate. Suppose sometime it sets and never appears in the east again. Such a thought would have put anyone in a panic and a frantic search for a remedy and a salvation.

One would imagine that there would be much to do in the way of sacrifices, rituals, prayers, and promises officiated and offered by the elders and seers designed to mollify and propitiate the power behind the scene so that it would change the course of the sun and bring back its light and heat and the full glory of its dawns and twilights. Then the always hopeful, in spite of the bleakness of the leafless forest, of a dearth of life, of a coffin of ice, would deck whatever abode they had with green and red and spread upon the tables some of their surplus as they waited for the outcome of their appeasements of their gods.

And one can imagine on or about four days after what one today knows as the winter solstice, a chilled citizen of that northern clime would by some crude clock discover and report to the watchful that the sun had not only not retreated farther to the south but in fact inched perceptibly to the north. Such a report would have indicated that the gods had heard their prayers and had decided to return the sun to thaw their land and to assure them of the light of life and of its comfort and warmth and would have thereby initiated within the community a celebration of the event in which goodwill, brotherhood, gladness, cheer, and charity reigned during a festival of feasts.

I have seen scenes in history books of serfs flailing grain in the 15th century, of serfs cultivating a field with a harrow in the 13th century, of laborer generations ago scything hay, cradling wheat, shocking wheat and hay, just as I did under the mentor-ship of my grandfather on a farm in Summers County in the Twenties and Thirties. And I have known the sincere and joyous embrace of the winter solstice with its promise that the pinch and chill, the snow and ice, the mud and muck of winter were on the way out and spring was on the way in.

I remember the depth of winter particularly when dinner-time came. The meal was served in the kitchen, the only room with heat except the living room where the fireplace with back-log and forelog and logs in between radiated heat and light and attracted after supper outstretched palms and chilled backsides of everyone in residence. The kitchen was lighted by a kero-sene lamp that gave not much more illumination than a bottle of lightning bugs. But 'twas enough to reveal the dishes of the meat, vegetables, fruits, and grains harvested and preserved to sustain the family until spring. From a hilltop one viewing the farm house could detect only that faint light from fireplace and lamp, a speck of lame light in a vast ocean of darkness. Like all life, we hunkered down, drew close to the fireplace, and await-ed the drama and the eventual demise of winter and reprise of spring.

I never read of the newborn Jesus having to spend his first night in a manger that I do not remember those dark evenings when I went to the barn with lantern to feed the stock waiting patiently for hay and corn. I would climb to the loft and fork down hay and open the grain box, select a number of ears of corn and distribute the hay to the cows and fill the horses' man-gers with corn. The box with the corn in it was the sort of box Mary's baby was laid for the night.

It was politically wise for the church fathers to select the win-ter solstice as the birthdate of Christ, just as it was politically wise and necessary for the bishops at Nicaea to vote to accept the belief that Jesus was God; for without that divinity attributed to him, Christianity would probably have long since been a foot-note of history.

Christ's birthday is occasion enough for celebration, but even more basic is the return of the sun—for without the sun all life would freeze and resolve itself into mere ice.

Crusade of Secularism to Defeat Moslem Terrorism

THE CHRISTIANS AND THE MOSLEMS have warred conventionally against one another since the rise in the Arabian Peninsula of militant Mohammendanism in the 7th Century. In 732 at Tours, France, Charles Martel thwarted the greatest threat to Christendom by Moslems, who had conquered their way across North Africa, crossed the Mediterranean Sea at Gibraltar, invaded Spain then France and there met defeat. The loss of Spain in 1492 still rankles in Moslems' memories.

In 1529, Solyman, an Ottoman Turk and Moslem, besieged the city of Vienna on his way into the heartland of Christendom. "But the small Austrian garrison, valorously supported by the undaunted burghers, beat off the Moslem host and obliged Solyman to raise the siege."

In 1389, at Kossovo, in the heart of the Balkans, Murad, an Ottoman, routed Orthodox Christians under Lazar of Serbia. Both Murad and Lazar perished in the struggle. But the indelible imprint of Mohammad and his teachings was an aftermath of Kossovo that persists to this day and was evident when Yugoslavia fell apart and the Orthodox Christians and Moslems set upon one another with murderous and pitiless assault.

In Medieval times, Christians had evolved a faith that was to them so certain the Church, which had nurtured it, brooked no challenge to it. In fact, those who differed with the faith of the Church were subjected to interrogation by torture and if found guilty of heresy, were put to death by burning at the stake, a horrible penalty for following one's belief.

But the Enlightenment birthed by the Renaissance and the heritage from the Greek and Roman thinkers and writers of secular minds—which heritage was preserved by Moslems and restored to the West by the Crusaders—tended to undermine the theological and ideological certainties of the Church. The result has been in the West the residue of Inquisitional forces has been slowly but surely weakened by science, secular scholarship, and common sense—Charles Darwin having dealt the Coup de Grace to the threat of theocratic hegemony.

This evolution in the West from religious absolutism to separation of church and state—mankind's greatest victory in the history of secularism and the freedom of conscience—is a phenomenon that is mostly alien in the lands of Mohammedanism. In Islamic lands today, the medieval aspect of the West's evolution from Taliban-mindedness to the 1st Amendment—is as fanatical in Taliban adherents as it was in the Christian clerics that condemned the mystical teenager Joan of Arc to die in flames.

The Moslem's answer to secularism is suicidal bombers that take their lives and all the other lives that stand in their way of making a statement for Allah. They do it in the belief it is what Allah demands and for the reward doing it will bring to them.

Western secularists believe that the Moslem bombers are misled. They are misled because science and knowledge and common sense evidence that there is no god, no heaven and hell, and no reward but death for those who sacrifice their lives to subject children and women and the aged to the deadly effects of detonated explosives. It's inexplicable that anyone of any religion can, declaring it's God's will, kill hundreds of others of mankind in an instant to gain a reward he or she believes will assure them of paradise forever. But it is the mindset the West is up against.

How does a nation defend itself against such a mindset and its terrorism? In Europe, the place of adoption of Christianity and the birthplace of the Inquisition, the cathedrals have become mainly tourists' attractions. The land of the Vatican is becoming secular, while South America and Africa, the lands of the uneducated and poor, have become the hope of the Vatican. The change in Europe has been through education in ageless secular knowledge—the basis of secular culture and of the subversion of absolutism—and through a betterment of the living conditions of the people of Europe.

The West is now, relative to the Moslem world, a super power. No Moslem nation can oppose it militarily with hope of defeating it. So the Moslems have innovated. They have brainwashed with religion many of their citizens to believe to bomb themselves into oblivion along with large numbers of infidels will be the way to paradise and all the pleasures therein. Apparently, a combination of this belief and patriotism is enough to induce them to do the deed.

Secularism's crusade must be to disabuse the Moslem world of its absolutist beliefs. The means are education and financial help and the West's living in a way that is admirable. Just as the European nations have secularized notably since the Age of Faith, so has the number of unbelievers increased statistically in this nation and alarmingly so from the view of Fundamentalists. Even though there are pockets of creationists in Europe and this nation, the change to secularism, although slow, has been sure. And doubtlessly will continue.

As education has spread and income has increased giving people the opportunity to acquire the knowledge of the ages and to have the time to learn alone, faith has faltered. There are few in Europe and this nation today who are not puzzled and shocked by the mindset of suicide bombers or outraged by the barbarities of Moslem religious laws. And there are few who do not look back on the Inquisition with disbelief, and there are many who view Fundamentalists as know-nothings.

The war on terrorism militarily is unwinnable, so long as the Moslems fight and die believing with a certainty that a heaven of pleasures, forever, awaits their sacrifices. It can be won by a Secular Crusade that employs enlightening education and economic betterment, the only weapons that can succeed in disabusing Moslem extremists and their heirs of the beliefs that inspire them to war with suicide.

This may take five hundred years, but better the expenditure of centuries of patience than billions in treasure and thousands in troops. So the strategy is to withdraw our forces, shore up our defenses against bombers, dedicate ourselves to build a stronger nation through education, economic justice, and moral discipline and let what has happened in the West take its course in Islam. Iran already is beset with citizens in the streets. It may be the harbinger of a more liberal nation.

This nation fought a fratricidal war that sacrificed nearly a million of its sons over a racial and economic issue that had its origin two hundred years before it was resolved somewhat by that war. Today, that issue is all but mute: Now that the presidency of this nation is in the hands of an African-American. The secularization of the Islamic World and the West is the only reasonable means of victory.

Hoist with One's Own Petard

THE TITLE IS A METAPHOR from Shakespeare and it means ruined by one's own devices. Such appears to be the destiny of the Catholic Church in Ireland. Christianity came to Ireland in the 5th Century, and the Catholic Church has had a religious relationship with the people of that tragic country since. That is until 1979 when Pope John Paul II visited Ireland and a third of the population turned out and 200,000 young people attended a special Mass. Since then the church's relationship with the populace has deteriorated precipitously. "In 1970, 90 percent of the Irish identified themselves as Catholic and almost the same number went to Mass once a week; now the figure for Mass attendance is closer to 25 percent." (The quote is from an article that appeared in the July 15, 2006 edition of the Saturday Gazette-Mail[2], and the other information in this article are taken therefrom.)

What happened? First, cynicism set in when it was discovered two of the Irish church's most charismatic leaders, Bishop Eamon Casey of Galway and the Rev. Michael Cleary, Dublin's singing priest, both of whom had entertained the faithful during the visit of the Pope—had violated their vow of celibacy. Casey was father of a son by an American woman and had attempted to cover up with church funds. Cleary had fathered

---

2 Charleston, West Virginia, Sunday Gazette-Mail newspaper

two children and had an abusive relationship with his house-keeper. Secondly, the worldwide revelation priests had for years assaulted altar-boys and had in general involved themselves in non-celibate activities.

But the coup de grace, the final blow, to the church was Ireland became rich. Today, Ireland is the European Union's second wealthiest nation per capita, second only to Luxembourg. The opium of the masses is no longer the church. It is riches and the independence that riches bring. The masses no longer grow potatoes to see them through the winter. Now they have money in the bank to see them through the winter. Thus, they do not look to the church as they once did, when the potatoes were gone. And with the church's loss of respect of the faithful and with the faithful's need of it undermined by wealth, the church has lost its authority and its rule over the masses and its influence in the making of Ireland's laws in accordance with Rome.

"Through most of the 20th century, Ireland was poor, backward and deeply Catholic. Irish Catholicism tended to be a particularly harsh and unforgiving variety. Worse than the ordinary miserable childhood is the miserable Irish childhood, and worse yet is the miserable Irish Catholic childhood," wrote Frank McCourt, whose memoir, "Angela's Ashes," resonated among many Irish Catholics on both sides of the Atlantic.

The worse the poverty and hardships of a tribe, the harsher and more unforgiving is its religion. One needs only to read Leviticus to learn how harsh was Jehovah's commandments and the penalties for violation of them: Death by stoning for adultery; death for disobeying a parent; death for working on the Sabbath; and death for worshipping any other God than Jehovah.

Europe, where once men and women were burned at the stake for heresy—that is, for having a faith different from that proclaimed by the Pope or for having no religion at all—is a nearly secular continent now. Education has enlightened and liberalized the people, and wealth has given them a sense of freedom from dogma. The cathedrals faith built are tourists' attractions now and are relatively empty of believers on worship days.

In this nation, the fundamentalists are concerned. They are concerned because they have supported capitalism, and it has produced great wealth. They know in their hearts great wealth undermines religion. How does a youth who has a trust of a billion dollars react when he is told to obey his parents because it is one of the Ten Commandments? He is more likely to obey the trustee and tell his parents to go jump in the lake. The Commandments, with the exception of murder, theft, and false witness, are meaningless to a man with a billion dollars. And he has infinitely less reason to break those three than does a man in poverty. Wealth is the solvent of family cohesion.

The Ten Commandments evolved from tribal experiences over centuries. The tribal leaders and thinkers in view of their experiences and the history of their tribe and other tribes decided what a member of the tribe should not do in order to assure the stability, safety, welfare, and future of the tribe. To give the Commandments authority, the elders attributed the origin of them to Jehovah and their revelation to God's creation in his image, namely man, through Moses. Today, some of them are obsolete. Who keeps the Sabbath holy today in the manner prescribed in that Commandment? What Christian worships only the God of Moses? And who does not covet or imitate the Joneses? Madison Avenue is in the business of breeding covetousness.

The fundamentalists are slowly but surely hoisting themselves with their own petard. Many of them are wealthy, and wealth not only subverts belief and conduces one to indulgences but is an obstacle to entering the Kingdom. They insist on believing the inerrancy of the Bible, an incredible presumption in view of a plethora of miracles, contradictions, and myths therein. They believe the Creation story literally in spite of the mountain of evidence to the contrary. And they maintain without any evidence whatever there is a heaven and a hell in an after life.

Sooner or later the majority of people or their children will come to know the truth; that is, the Bible is not inerrant, the story of Creation is a fable, and humans are a species in a chain and a spread of species originating from a common source that awoke four billion years ago. Nature has writ in the genes the way for humankind.

I wrote this after Shock and Awe but not long after. I am pleased to read what I wrote in view of the outcome of Bush and Cheney's response to 9/11. We lost the war. Thousands killed and wounded and a trillion of treasure spent. The liberal view then would have saved this nation and the world much in life and treasure.

Jesus's Treasonous Teachings

I<small>F NATIONAL SECURITY IS THE</small> end, the question is whether or not war is a realistic means to it. Karl Rove and this nation's Commander in Chief believe war without question is the means to it and consider anyone who doesn't think war is the right means is thinking treasonously.

The following is Rove's assessment of conservatives and liberals' reaction to 9/11: "Conservatives saw the savagery of 9/11 attacks and prepared for war; liberals saw the savagery of the 9/11 attacks and wanted to prepare indictments and offer therapy and understanding to our attackers. In the wake of 9/11, conservatives believed it was time to unleash the might and power of the United States military against the Taliban; in the wake of 9/11, liberals believed it was time to submit a petition. ... Conservatives saw what happened to us on 9/11 and said: We will defeat our enemies. Liberals saw what happened to us and said: We must understand our enemies."

So we now have some notion of what consequences we face as a result of deciding war is a realistic means. Where is our security more than two years after unleashing our military might? The reports that filter through this administration's censorship are that the Taliban in Afghanistan is still killing American troops and the U.S. backed government is shaky; that the masterminds of 9/11 are still at large; that the shock-and-awe attacks in Iraq did not shock and awe the insurgents, who are still increasing and killing and wounding by daily bombings our troops and everyone else supporting them; and that there is no foreseeable end to the war in Afghanistan or Iraq or peace there so long as Rove's view prevails.

Furthermore, this nation has been weakened by the war. In addition to the dead and wounded, there is the cost in treasure, there is the loss of international respect, there is the loss of will in this nation to continue the war, and there is the malevolence—a cancer that will grow and affect us—created by the invasion, death, destruction and occupation visited, willy-nilly, upon the people of Iraq. No Iraqi whose family was blown to bits, and which atrocity was dismissed as collateral damage, is likely ever to feel good will toward this nation nor will his kin for generations to come. War is an extreme means that engenders extreme reactions and etches indelibly its horrors in the minds of its victims. America's secular bible should include the admonition: God's mills grind slowly but surely.

So, suppose this nation had wanted to "prepare indictments and offer therapy and understanding for our attackers," as Rove sarcastically and falsely alleged liberals had wished to do. Where would we be with regard to national security? No one knows, but one can speculate with some solid grounds for the speculation because Rove and Bush's solution has been tried and found wanting.

If the world is ever to know a time when the resolution of conflicts between nations can be settled short of war, it will be when the United Nations, or an equivalent entity, hears the complaints and rules for the complaining nation or for the defending nation. Otherwise, war will ever be an addiction of nations ruled by warmongers. Thus, had this nation turned to the United Nations for relief, compensation, and future security and had pledged to it the whole of its might and resources in furtherance thereof, I suspect we would be further along in realizing some justice and satisfaction for the deaths, wounds, and costs resulting from the horror of 9/11—and a future more secure.

Consider that we had mandated the creation of a blue-ribbon commission to determined why a few Muslims hated us so fiercely they were willing to plan for years patiently and then to sacrifice their lives in order to hurt this nation grievously. And from that commission we learned the whys of the attack or at least a sane avenue toward a rapprochement. Then we could alter our policies and pursue others more compatible with the views of Muslims or make a good faith attempt to compromise the differences just as we would with regard to our neighbors who complained of some irritants to them caused by what we did or did not do. If compromise was not an option, then the civilized recourse would be to take the issue to an international court. War in view of its rewards relative to its costs often gains neither side anything finally.

Rove sneers when he suggests liberals "offer therapy" to the perpetrators of 9/11. He and his kind have no conception of trying to understand their enemies, and they give no consideration to taking steps to heal the wounds we have inflicted by our global political, economic, and military actions calculated to aggrandize us.

Rove and Bush's reaction is Old Testament morality: an eye for an eye. And if the innocents get in the way of the implementation of such morality, the perpetrators justify the slaughter of the innocents as a regrettable concomitant of warfare—defined as collateral damage.

Ask any religious fundamentalist to characterize this nation, and he will in a nanosecond declare that it is a Christian nation, including our born-again president. One hears that and despairs in view of the chasm of contradictions between what Christ taught and what this nation's history is and what manner of history it is making. Christ taught and lived peace and even refused to defend himself. Christ taught forgiveness even for those who crucified him. He taught returning goodness for badness. He taught storing up riches cripples the spirit. He taught every stranger is a neighbor. And he taught if a neighbor is in need of understanding and therapy, one should supply them.

If Christ presides at Judgment Day and the record there includes Rove's latest manifestation of his soul's condition, Rove will have a difficult time squaring it with the condition of the soul of him who spoke the Sermon on the Mount, which one assumes he has read. For one can find in that soul's manifestation ample evidence that when one suffers a wound, he should not return evil for evil but should return understanding and therapy. The resort to war is an expediency—the forfeiture of a long term solution for a short term gain. The undertaking of understanding and therapy is a principled investment in a lasting solution. Bush the Christian conducts foreign affair as a barbarian.

It is a puzzle and an enigma—considering Christ's teachings—how fundamentalist Christians can align and ally themselves with politicians of Rove's stripe or how they can countenance consumerism, homophobia, and the death penalty as well as approve this administration's reaction to 9/11. If a Christian offered understanding and therapy in Christ's name to one of the enemy or conspired to do so, he would likely end up incarcerated and interrogated, if not imprisoned indefinitely.

For a Christian or anyone else to take seriously Jesus's teachings would undoubtedly lead to his actions being regarded as treasonous. America claims to be a Christian nation. But I doubt that Christ, were he to come again would, after a day of observation, agree.

Let's Put God in Capitalism and Congress

THE CRY FROM THE RIGHT is to put God back in the classroom. Taking God out of the classroom according to the loudest voices of the Republican rightwing has resulted in every evil that besets this country from teenage pregnancies to school slaughters, and putting Him back would solve all problems. Prayer in the classroom is a panacea for what ails America. Such an assertion is a mountain of simplism and a desert of silliness.

Newt Gingrich: "God has been driven out of the classroom, and we have seen the result in a secular atheistic system in which God is not allowed to exist." This is nothing but reckless, demagogic bombast. Who has driven God out of the classroom or from any room or any place? Where is the sinister, secular atheistic system Newt warns us of? How has God been exterminated? If He doesn't exist, where is He? Preachers shout from pulpits at every opportunity God is omnipotent, omnipresent, and omniscient. How can puny man push such a God around? Gingrich doesn't care how illogical his rhetoric just so long as he lifts his listeners and lays every national ill at the doorsteps of liberals and humanists.

Tom Delay: "What message is sent when it is illegal to pray in schools? ... The message too many American children receive is that God does not exist or is not important in our lives. This rejection of God must change. Liberals demagogue tragedies like school shootings to push their left-wing agenda. But the big problem in America is not gun ownership. The big problem is the abandonment of God in the public arena. In the battle for our culture, we all need to understand that you cannot stand up for America – you need to kneel down for America and stand up for God."

When did it become illegal to pray in school? Never. Anyone at anytime can pray in school so long as his prayer does not interrupt the teacher's presentation. Any number of students at any time any where can join in group prayer so long as it is done on their time and not school time. Who, pray tell, delivers to children the message God does not exist? How can God be abandoned? Delay talks theological nonsense.

From the doings of capitalists and Congress, children, particularly poor children, certainly feel that God has abandoned them, that God's Son's visit to man was in vain and that His message has fallen on deaf ears in the halls of power and in the temples of the money-changers.

It is inconceivable, if Jesus spoke for God, gun ownership is compatible with His will. Guns are created to kill. There is no other use for them. Both bibles, the Hebrew and the Gentile, prohibit killing; and Jesus taught that one should not only not kill but that one should not even be angry with his fellowman, lest he be damned, and that he should embrace evil, turn the other cheek, and walk the extra mile.

What arrogance to suggest that God needs man to stand up for Him! God needs nothing. It is man that needs everything. The "kneel down for America and stand up for God" is without doubt some hired hack's demagogic phrase hatched in a midnight session to put words in DeLay's mouth to wow the mindless.

If one listens to DeLay and if one follows his voting record, one can find absolutely nothing in his words or his votes to indicate he ever read the Sermon on the Mount or any other words of Christ. He is mean-spirited, and he cannot even comprehend that inasmuch as one does for the least he does for Christ.

Newt Gringrich and Tom DeLay are devotees and legatees of capitalism, a system whose sole purpose is to produce wealth, to serve mammon, to reap profits, to exploit peasants, and to acquire worldly power. It lays up treasures and stores mountains of wares and things that are subject to rust, thieves, and moths; its heart is in its treasures, and it rewards the faithful with untold wealth, a substance that is an obstacle to salvation so large it is as difficult to overcome as for a camel to pass through the eye of a needle. So said the God who Newt and DeLay say that liberals have abandoned when in fact it is they who have abandoned God, as well as affronted Him by their worship of the Golden Calf Capitalism. Where is God in capitalism or in Congress, except in the token recognition given in prayer before sessions dedicated to worldly designs?

Christ's message is nothing if not one of cooperation, sacrifice, and charity. A Christianity compatible with Christ's teachings is the antithesis of capitalism and of the stance of Congress and the courts and the military. There is nothing in America of a nationally institutional kind that is not anti-Christ. The economy is run by the rich, for the rich, and of the rich. The Congress is bought by the rich, for the rich, and of the rich. The courts rule for the powerful, for the status quo, and against the people. The media, with a few exceptions, peddle porn, soft and hard, and pander and prostitute for capital. And the military is designed to protect and maintain the rich and powerful and to insulate them from foreign threats as well as from domestic insurrections.

There is more God in the heart of a teacher doing her best to educate a classroom of students than in the hearts of all the members of the House, the Senate, and the directors of all of corporate America. The need for God is not in the classroom but in the House and Senate and in corporate boardrooms.

Rather than prayer in schools and the display of the Ten Commandments, I suggest two remedies for Godless America. One is the publishing everywhere of a precis of the Sermon on the Mount, the very heart of Christianity and God's message to the world.

"Be humble. Be merciful. Seek righteousness. Keep a pure heart. Make peace. Love your enemies. Forgive those who wrong you. Turn the other cheek. Give to the poor. Give alms in secret. Pray in your closet. Serve one master, namely, God. Enter the strait gate and tread the narrow way. Beware of false Prophets and know them by their fruits. And be perfect as God is perfect.

"Swear no oaths. Judge not. Store not up worldly treasures. Do not strain at a gnat and swallow a camel. Note not the mote in another's eye. And take no thought for tomorrow, for sufficient unto the day is the evil thereof."

Second, I propose that, to compete with auto plates that call the public's attention to John 3:16 and Acts something or the other and to counter the call for prayer in the classroom, a plate be designed that reads Matthews 6: 6. And since I feel certain few recall what Jesus taught in that scripture, I will remind them and others who cannot think beyond prayer in the schools and on the streets and at every place where the righteous can display their piety.

"But thou, when thou prayest, enter into thy closet, and when thou hast shut the door, pray to thy Father which is in secret; and thy Father which seeth in secret shall reward thee openly."

Suburban Sins

WHAT IS GOD'S WILL? OFTEN, it seems, His will is the will of whoever defines His will. Many say that the Bible is the fullest expression of God's will but usually only in so far as it accords with how they interpret it. Sociobiologists have concluded God's will is nature's message encoded in the genes of man discerned by man as conscience and further the message's sole design is to perpetuate the species. That is, morality is the evolutionary creation of nature, a genetic legacy, for the single purpose of assuring the health and welfare of man and of the environment that sustains him. Thus, to live in harmony with it is virtue, to live in dissonance with it is sin.

Henry David Thoreau (1817-1862) said man's body is a temple, and every decision made by the mind of that body is a moral decision. So the life of Thoreau was the sum of its decisions, a reflection of his morality, the essence of which morality and philosophy was "Simplify, Simplify." And was there ever a man who followed his philosophy, it was he. If Thoreau, who said man only needed to labor six weeks to provide all his needs for the year, were to return suddenly unaware of what "progress" has come since his demise, he would be shocked stone still, if not lifeless, when he looked upon the intensity of the rage to haste, the extent of the rape and pillage of the land, the obscene luxury in which many live, the outrageous superfluity dubbed necessity and the gross waste in the wake of the wealthy.

For hundreds of years Christians have been indifferent to the fate of the environment, owing principally to Jehovah's injunction that man multiply, fill the earth, and subdue it. Never has a command so thoroughly, energetically, and enthusiastically been heard, read, and rendered. And Adam's progeny, oblivious, amoral and dumb as dice, continue apace to multiply and subdue and subvert the very origin of their being and in the process commit patricide and matricide in order to fill barns with stuff subject to moths, rust, and thieves, dedicating as well their hearts to the treasures in their barns.

But there is a voice in the wilderness, a Christian minister who questions Genesis, and has the temerity to say: "We either support this life-giving, nurturing presence of God's spirit, or we make everything act against it." And he further opines: "Sin in the Bible is anything that is against God's holy will. And God's holy will is to nurture and to enhance life."

The headline of the article from which the above quotes come is: "Thou shalt not... drive an SUV?" The writer of the headline believes that one can reasonably infer from the minister's concept of God's will that driving a gas-guzzling vehicle is detrimental to the environment and therefore wrong. If the minister's reading of God's will is correct and the writer's inference is logical, then one can argue that driving an SUV is a sin, maybe not a mortal one, but a sin nevertheless—which is a conclusion that carries a can of corollaries.

If a SUV is an abomination in the eyes of God, what is an ATV or a snowmobile, a watermobile, or any other kind of mobile that requires the polluting of the earth to furnish fuel for it and further pollutes the earth in the operation of it? What about aircraft and the observation that if God wanted man to fly, He would have provided him with wings? What is man's hurry?

If he hadn't in his greedy mind converted time to money, he wouldn't need to rush around the world burying nuts here and there until he has no need of nuts or anything else.

And then there is the question of food. If God's will is that man do nothing that does not nurture and enhance life, what is a reasonable guess as to God's judgment regarding a Big Mac or MacThis or a MacThat or any of the many other bun-caressed meat patties lavished and larded with libido-loving layers of whatever, all of which, if nothing else, tend to distort the temple that is man?

And what about drink?—aside from alcoholic beverages, which have long ago been declared evil. Surely, in the beginning water was the beverage of choice, primarily I suppose because there was nothing else to drink. Adam and Eve had no wine cellar. But look at now. Who drinks water except prissy men and women who can afford to import it from some sequestered spring in the Alps? From the Alps because man has polluted the springs everywhere else? Athletes drink Gatorade, a man-made liquid touted to be far superior to God's drink, and boys and girls drink oceans of Coke, Pepsi, Dr. Pepper, and a dozen other brands of pop, all of which do little to refresh, nurture, and enhance life. At least, not my life and I suspect not theirs.

What would Thoreau, think of a man who spent $40 million to build a house for him, his wife, and so far two children and after it was built decided it needed an addition? When I ask this question, I have in mind that Thoreau built and lived in a house that cost him somewhere in the neighborhood of a few $100 in today's money. Consider what would be the impact on the earth if every family on it had at least a million-dollar house with all that goes with it. Think of the heating, the cooling, the sewage, the pollution, the degradation of the environment in the building, and the upkeeping of it all. Think of sins and of a multiplicity of them.

Diogenes, the philosopher who roamed the earth looking for an honest man, had an estate that consisted of the clothes on his back and a wooden bowl. He cast the bowl away as superfluous when he saw a child cup his hands to drink. He taught man's happiness is best promoted by the decrease of his wants, rather than the increase of his income. Only Christ and a few others strange souls would hear Diogenes and not consider him insane. Certainly, suburbanites would have him in a straight jacket with little delay.

I for one am elated to learn the church fathers at last have begun to see nature is God's supreme creation, that its maintenance is indispensable to the nurture and welfare of man and that any act that degrades it is certainly an affront to God and against his will. And a sin. Amen.

The Mess the Myth Has Made

ONCE UPON A TIME IN the dawn of civilization somewhere at the crossroads of his world, a human with a poetic imagination decided to describe fancifully how he and all his brethren and sisters and all organic and inorganic things came to be. A God, he imagined, created man in His image and woman from a rib of man and enjoined man to multiply and subdue the earth and have dominion over it and every living thing that moved on it. The poet had no notion of what an impact his poetry would have on following generations and on God's creation.

Centuries later a human who suspected that the poetic myth wasn't what really happened took ship and sailed to many lands with his notebook, and after years of scientific scrutiny of nature concluded that man wasn't created in a day but that man evolved over millions of years from a simple-celled something to a complex animal with sense and conscience. And that he was not created in the image of a God but in the image of nature. The scientist had a notion of the impact of his study and the controversy it would engender. But he told the truth as he saw it.

Today, more people believe the poet's myth than believe the scientist's evolutionary theory. And thus more people believe that the earth was made primarily for man's consumption and convenience regardless of whether such a belief is to the detriment of all else or not. As a result one species, namely, man has made and is making a mess out of the good earth that God put him on or on which he evolved. He is not only jeopardizing his very existence by carving out of the earth what he wants instead of just what he needs but endangering the existence of all other species most of which are content to get just what they need from earth and are circumspect in the quantities that they store up.

Man knows no limit to the variety of his wants or to the quantities of them, particularly since many of his brothers are in the business of producing what is not needed, and an army of others are in the business of convincing man he cannot do without what he doesn't need if he really wants to be happy. And from all this business the earth suffers, and the birds and butterflies suffer, and all else that is not man suffers except those men who provide the insatiable wants of men in power. They suffer from over work and inequitable pay.

The man who believes he was made in the image of God and that he is different in kind from all other life has little compunction with regard to how he exploits and plunders the creation he religiously believes God made in days and exhorted him to dominate and subdue along with every other living thing on earth.

But the man who believes that he is blood kin to all other life, that he evolved over millions of years from swamp cells to a human and that his future health is tied inextricably with the health of all other species, plant and animal, has compunctions of a moral kind and also has concerns related to the question of whether or not his kind can have a future without a future for all life. The earth to an evolutionist is a biosphere, and the toll for any species is a toll for man. Ask not for whom the bell tolls.

As world population has doubled and as the global economy has expanded sevenfold over the last half-century, our claims on the Earth have become excessive. We are asking more of the

Earth than it can give on an ongoing basis. We are harvesting trees faster than they can regenerate, overgrazing rangelands and converting them into deserts, overpumping aquifers and draining rivers dry. On our cropland soil erosion exceeds new soil formation, slowly depriving the soil of its inherent fertility. We are taking fish from the ocean faster than they can reproduce.

Throughout history, humans have lived on the Earth's sustainable yield—the interest from its natural endowment. But now we are consuming the endowment itself. In ecology, as in economics, we can consume principal along with interest in the short run but in the long run it leads to bankruptcy.

The poet who envisioned man as a semi-god, the child of the only God, and immune to the consequences of profligacy in the uses of the home his Father prepared for him—if he is looking on to what is happening to that creation—should be concerned if not in a panic state over its welfare. But from what a man reads today, the poet's successors are complacent and smug and doubt not but that whatever they do with the creation is pre-approved by Him, who told them to use it and to procreate a multi-progeny to use even more of it, ad infinitum.

The successors to the man who shocked the creationists can see the handwriting on the wall. What it says is that time is running out for those whose god is consumption and whose religion is that of the poet that spun the myth that has led to this mess.

To prevent catastrophe to the entire world, men who have must share it and share a painful amount of it. And populations must be stabilized, soil erosion must be contained, soil rehabilitation must be enhanced, water use must be conserved, carbon dioxide emissions must be reduced, habitat destruction must be mitigated, Earth's endowment must be preserved, and Earth must be honored as the mother of us all and the only nurture, physical and spiritual, of us all.

The Nature of Fundamentalism

"FUNDAMENTALISM REALLY CANNOT HELP ITSELF—IT is absolutist and can compromise with nothing, not even democracy. It is not surprising that immediately after the Islamic fundamentalist attack on the World Trade Center and the Pentagon, two prominent Christian fundamentalists were reported to have accounted it a justifiable punishment by God for our secularism, our civil libertarianism, our feminists, our gay and lesbian citizens, our abortion providers and everything and everyone else that their fundamentalist belief condemns. In thus honoring the foreign killers of almost 3000 Americans as agents of God's justice, they established their own consanguinity with the principle of righteous warfare in the name of all that is holy, and gave their pledge of allegiance to the theocratic ideal of government of whatever sacred text."

The Jews believe they are God's chosen people and the Holy Land was conveyed to them by a divine deed with general warranty title in perpetuity. The Mormons are so certain their theology is identical with God's will they send their youth all over the world to save everybody they can from his and her theological ignorance or willfulness. The Baptists know without question that all others' faiths and philosophies are in error, if not the workings of the Devil, and that unless the lost listen to them and come into their church, hell is their inevitable habitation for eternity. Jehovah's Witnesses believe only a select group of them will see heaven and apparently no one else. And the Catholics have no less a conviction in the uniqueness and divine origin of their faith.

Islamic fundamentalists are so certain of their theology and so certain of their knowledge of the mind of God that they explode themselves and many others to bloody bits with the expectation that they will forever thereafter reside in a heavenly, air-conditioned oasis inhabited for their pleasure by dark-eyed maidens.

And E. L. Doctorow has made clear in the quote above from "Why We Are Infidels" that the Christian Right or the evangelical fundamentalists are no less certain that they know the workings of God's justice and know God inspired and instructed the Saudi fanatics to take down the WTC on 9/11—in order to let America know in an unequivocal manner that He disapproved of its secularism, etc. In asserting that the killing of 3000 Americans was God's justifiable retribution, fundamentalists "established their own consanguinity with the principle of righteous warfare in the name of all that is holy, and gave their pledge of allegiance to the theocratic ideal of government of whatever sacred text." That is, they have an affinity with and allegiance to theocracy.

What would Thomas Jefferson learn could he have knowledge of where America has gone and what America has become? He would learn on return very quickly that America is a corpocracy, or plutocracy, ruled by the money of corporations and by those made rich by corporations that have expropriated an inordinate and unjust share of the value labor has created and that it was led currently [George W. Bush] by a confessed-alcoholic who found Jesus but who apparently never read the Sermon on the Mount. And that fundamentalists, descendants of the Pharisees, had the ear and mind of the 43rd president, who recklessly is undermining the wall separating church and state, the safeguard Jefferson spent his life trying to establish in view of his knowledge of the European terrorists arising from established religion and its warfare and Inquisition.

Since the Christian Right has through its leaders expressed the opinion that the horrors of 9/11 were the result of God's wrath resulting from this nation's sins, it seems reasonable that one with no affinity with the Christian Right may under the aegis of the First Amendment express his views as to why God was provoked to wrath and retribution. First, He was provoked by the hypocrisy of this nation's claim to be Christian when it violates every tenet, every teaching, of God's son, every day. Second, He was provoked by this nation's arrogance in the belief that its every action was manifest destiny, divinely sanctioned, and that every other nation's actions were, if adverse to this nation's profit, the work of the devil. Third, by this nation's belief that all other life, plant and animal, was its preserve and legacy to pillage, plunder, and consume with abandon for its profit, comfort, and delight. Fourth, by this nation's belief that God upon day's end took note in his journal of what happened in America and Israel and took no note of what happened in any other nation on the ground that no other nation had any of His concern.

And lastly, by this nation's efforts to frustrate the just goals of the exploited poor and oppressed of the world by the expenditure of billions to fund fascist thugs with weapons of destruction and by the tacit mandate to use whatever means necessary to defeat the yearnings of the landless and powerless for a better world.

Fundamentalism's absolutism is its comfort and complacency, but it is also its arrogance and pride, the elements of the first of the Cardinal Sins and the seeds of its destruction. Faith forced upon another by violence or law is a Satanic presumption.

Perry Mann

The Far-Right's Relativism

THE FAR-RIGHT TALKS ABSOLUTES. IT believes every word in the Bible is the word of God and thus is inerrant. It also believes Jesus is the Son of God and of the same substance as God, the Father. Therefore, the Bible is a composite of absolutes. The Far-Right scolds the Liberal-Left and dubs its situational ethics and its lack of reverence for divine absolutes—as relativism. But on some issues even ultra-conservatives deal in relativism.

Gary Bauer, a former Republican presidential candidate and Christian, in response to the question "Would Jesus Torture?" answered as follows: "There are a lot of things Jesus wouldn't do because he is the son of God. I can't imagine Jesus being a Marine or a policeman or a bank president, for that matter. The more appropriate question is, 'What is a follower of Jesus permitted to do?'" Bauer's answer: "It depends."

On what does it depend? Bauer believes if the suspect is not a soldier but a terrorist who may have knowledge of an impending attack, then water-boarding is appropriate and even though it simulates drowning, is not torture.

Where are the words of God? Where are the moral absolutes? Bauer jettisoned them when he premised that Jesus was God and what Jesus would do was not relevant to the issue. Why are not the absolutes of the Sermon on the Mount pertinent to the issue of torture? They are not relevant to the Far-right because they are so morally challenging and so totally contrary to conservatives' politics. Thus, conservatives must neutralize them with sophistry. What Republican would give his riches to the poor and follow Jesus' way? Or would advocate turning the other cheek as a principle of international relations?

In both the Gospel of Matthew and Luke, Jesus takes to a mount and teaches a sublime morality. Whether he was God's son or just a man with a moral message, he is the foundation of Christianity. But Christians fall over themselves in working for and supporting the display of the Hebrew Bible's Ten Commandments on public or private land. However, it is egregiously strange Christians do not work for and support the display of the Beatitudes or want to build a monument on Mt. Everest or on any mountain or in any public square displaying the tenets of the Sermon on the Mount. Why?

Well, the why is easily answered by just a few words from the Sermon: Jesus blessed the meek, the merciful and the peacemakers; he said one should not only not kill but not be angry with his brother; he said one should not only not commit adultery but also he should not look upon woman with lust; he said eye for an eye should no longer be the law but it should be turn the other cheek, do good for evil and love your enemies and those who hate you; he said when giving alms, let not the left hand know what the right hand does; when praying go to a closet and shut the door; he said no man should swear an oath for any reason; he said that no man can serve two masters; he said judge not, lest one be judged by his judgment; and he said to him who would be perfect he should give all that he has to the poor and follow him.

But to Bauer and the Christians of the Right, the Sermon apparently is just so much God talk and not to be introduced as an inerrant way into humankind's marketplaces, politics, and homes. It is what God and his son taught but what they taught is to be guides and laws to Christian men and women—only under certain circumstances. To conservatives when they try to bridal liberals with their absolutes, the words are absolutes, but when they are faced with them, they take the tack that it depends.

Bauer's surrender to the call of relativism is not a first. In fact, one can go back to St. Paul and learn he set aside conforming to the Sermon for salvation and premised the way to salvation was through justification by faith. Not doing good works, not turning the other cheek and so forth, but just believing in Christ's death and resurrection.

Paul differed with Matthew. Paul taught that followers of Jesus did not have to keep the law of the Jews but were justified by faith. Matthew's Jesus taught differently: "Think not that I am come to destroy the law, or the prophets: I am not come to destroy, but to fulfill."

Martin Luther read the Sermon, looked into his heart and soul, and agonized over his lack of moral will to abide by it. So, he compromised and settled for faith as the way to salvation rather than doing good works and walking the extra mile. It was the Creed's victory over the Sermon.

The church fathers long ago recognized that a church based on the Sermon would never flourish because to abide by it would mandate, among other moral challenges, serving God and denying Mammon. So they evolved the Creed and made Jesus a God so that they could avoid the challenge of the Sermon and abide by the Creed, which required no moral sweat, in order to be saved and know eternal life.

Would Jesus torture? If there was such a man and if he taught what the Gospels declare he taught and lived, then without question, he would not torture. There would be no equivocation and no dependence upon circumstances.

Preachers Have a Vested Interest in Creationism

I HAVE READ THE CATHOLIC Church has conceded the earth is not the center of the universe and after four centuries has apologized for burning Giordano Bruno, a Dominican monk, at the stake for agreeing with Copernicus and has asked forgiveness for threatening to do the same to Galileo and forcing him to eat his words. I have also read the Pope has conceded Darwin was on to something and there is truth in the theory of evolution. The Baptists today, I surmise, concede the former but I read they without a dissenting voice adamantly reject the latter. In fact, a Baptist pastor on behalf of his flock has implied shootings by schoolchildren are the result of the teaching of evolution. Teaching it, he says, is "undermining their foundational values."

Why would the truth of earth's relatively insignificant position among the celestial bodies of the universe so disturb a church it would go so far as to burn a member for believing it. I suspect when the inquisitors were at Bruno to change his mind one of them pleaded: "But, Giordano, don't you realized that even if your position is true, it must not be admitted by the church, for it would undermine the foundational values of the children and then all hell would break loose." Giordano refused to recant and went bravely to his death and no more hell than usual broke loose.

The trouble with being dogmatic and arrogantly certain is when one's dogma is undermined; it is ever so much more difficult to admit one's error, particularly when one's livelihood and an institution's future are in the balance. The reason the Catholic Church burnt to death some of the great characters and minds of the ages is that its authority and power were threatened. It had a vested interest in ignorance and committed atrocities to perpetuate that ignorance. And so it is today with Baptists with regard to evolution. They have a vested interest in Creationism, and evolution threatens that interest. They have painted themselves into a theological corner with the dogma that every word in the Bible is literally true. If they had the power, I suspect some modern-day Giordanos would have met the same fate as the one of the 16th century.

My children grew up at the table, and I was there preaching, not just on Sunday but every day. My text invariably was politically liberal or theologically unorthodox or both. I deified FDR and castigated Hoover and all his tribe and I spoke reverently of Darwin and his theory and skeptically of Creationism and of much else in the New and Old Testaments. I did talk lovingly of Jesus and his message. However, neither of my children apparently is worse off for my having undermined Republican dogma or conventional religious beliefs. And If there is a heaven, I guess their chance will be as good as most earthlings wondering what this is all about.

As I see it, it is a disservice to children and to adults for a church and its pastors to announce with divine authority that all that is necessary for salvation is to believe literally every word of one book, namely, the Bible, to be baptized, to have faith, and accept the grace of God. Then, to sit back smugly and wait for the rapture, at which time they will ascend while the non-believers gnash their teeth in envy.

Such teachings subvert the will to investigate the meaning and mystery of life, to read and associate with all those great minds who have questioned conventional wisdom, orthodox dogma and Neanderthal notions, and to live vicariously with all the free spirits and secular saints who have revealed truth and created beauty in words and works.

I cut my teeth on Baptist theology. I know whereof I speak. And I suggest Baptists recognized in the long run their best interest is to stop dragging their theological feet, to reconcile with Darwin, and to stress Jesus's message more and easy salvation less.

Hope and Secular Mann

Hope without Heaven

A PASTOR ASSERTS UNEQUIVOCALLY: "IF Jesus were dead and in a tomb, as the case with all other religious leaders who ever lived, this world would be shrouded in hopelessness. Where the Christ is not known, there is little hope."

I cannot in good conscience respond to this assertion in the words that first crossed my mind upon reading it, for I would be unkind, and I would later regret belittling a man's faith. But such an egregiously erroneous exaggeration compels me to reply that I don't believe Christ arose from the dead, and I have hope and have hope abundantly, and so do many other people I know who believe as I do. And for that matter, countless souls who lived before Christ undoubtedly had hope, and so do millions of others of different faiths who live in this day. Does the good pastor really believe the only people on this earth who have hope are Christians? If so, he has sequestered himself in such theological confinement he knows little of the world outside his cloister.

Or he believes hope of life after death is the only basis for hope, and if he believes that, I can comprehend his hopelessness only as it regards his profession; preachers have a vested interest in a risen Christ and rightly so. They know the pews would be empty were it not for the Resurrection and the hope of heaven. So they must do what St. Paul does in Corinthians I, Chapter 15—the Scripture cited by the pastor—and what the pastor does in his article: Convince himself and others Christ arose from death, left the tomb, appeared to his disciples, and ascended to heaven.

One can argue reasonably to invest Christ with divinity is to minimize and degrade his life and words and to diminish the challenge of his example. In fact, to many of us, and certainly to me, it is an abiding inspiration that Christ did not rise from the dead and was not God's child any more than any other being is God's child, and that he undoubtedly was a man unique in his moral stature, who taught, in the words of Thomas Jefferson, a Unitarian, a "system or morality was the most benevolent and sublime ... ever taught."

Also one can complain: How can a mortal expect to be able to live in accordance with the moral code of a God? And thus take refuge in his mortality and justify his aberrant and deviant behavior, thereby. Moreover, he can through the mediations of the church wash away his sins and redeem himself through easy rites of belief and baptism and the gift of grace, all of which ecclesiastical ministrations and divine gifts require no moral sweat in the doing and abiding thereof.

What hope is there without belief in a risen Christ? There is always tomorrow, which is – to use street philosophy – the first day of the rest of one's life. Every day is as a thumb print: it is unique in some way. There is more often than not an unexpected joy and a chance to do some simple favor with no expectation of return, and sometimes there is the consequence of some past shortcoming for which there comes a day to pay. There is the weather of that day, and always the weather is of interest to man and beast: it has an effect that cheers or depresses, enhances or dampens the plans for the time. And so it is with seasons with their drama and beauty and tranquility and terror.

There is work. Always there is work, and if one's work is a union of one's avocation with his vocation, then he has heaven enough and hope sufficient. To be lost in one's occupation, to feel what one is doing is needful, to have adequate reward for the doing of it and at the end of day to have need of rest and a keen appetite — all of which conditions, engender a fervent wish to live another day.

There is love. That wonderful feeling that pervades one in the presence of the other. The parting and reunion. The planning and realizing. The anticipations and the consummations. And then that love that expects nothing in return. Love in all of its forms and expressions is conceived and nurtured by hope. To know love whether turbulent or tranquil is to have uplifting hope. In the back of the mind of everyone is the dream of enduring love, for no other state of the heart is so comforting.

There are children. In them is great hope. For therein are one's future and his immortality. Children who achieve, who honor parents, who become productive, responsible, disciplined, empathetic, and diligent adults and do all that bring beams to parents' faces, brighten the todays and tomorrows of their progenitors. Without another generation in the wing and with all that is left of mankind, moribund, on the world's stage, under such circumstances, then, the pastor could with reason talk about hopelessness but surely not in any other circumstances, even a buried Christ.

There is nature, God's greatest gift. There is no deceit in it, no ambiguity, no bribery, no discrimination, no allotment of rain measured by virtue and sin; no preferences on the basis of race, religion, sex, sexual orientation, or any other; no politics; no mitigation of the wages of waywardness, and no stinting of rewards of faithfulness to its mandates. Then there are all of its miracles and glories: sunsets and sunrises, the moon and its phases, fields and meadows, mountains and plains, skies and seas, flowers and birds, and the whole of creation.

Finally, there is death. An advent that should be no surprise to one who has reached adulthood and an advent one should consider inevitable and necessary in nature's plan. Man lives on life. Not a mouthful does he ingest but that some life has ended for his sustenance. It takes death to give life. Trees thrive on the leaves of yesteryears and on decayed parental trunks. So all of life lives on past generations. Thus, death is the final gift to progeny, a gift that is a sine qua non of life.

Why whine that without the prospect of life eternal after death there is no hope when hope is everywhere in spite of the death warrant that is concomitant with every birth notice? One should face it: Death is the end. But unless one has been inordinately damned by fate and has been inconceivably denied some measure of nature's benevolence, he can in that final moment of consciousness look back on the unique peaks and pits of his life and be content with the miracle of it all.

The Universal Kinship
of Humankind

GENESIS RELATES THAT A GOD created the earth, enhanced his creation with sky, clouds, stars, sun and moon; and in this setting, he populated it with a variety of species and crowned the creation with Adam and then Eve, who propagated a progeny that has, after centuries, settled on much of the space of the god's earth. If this narrative is true then all the settlers are kin, having a common ancestor. But it is probably a mystic's fantasy.

A better supported theory is Charles Darwin's evolution. He theorized that billions of years ago nature produced a spark of life, a spark that is the ancestor of all life, plant and animal, trees and humans. It happened by a process of mutations and natural selection. The evidence accumulated over the centuries by the scientific community has corroborated Darwin's theory with such certainty that there is no longer any doubt but that men and women everywhere on this earth today are the descendants of that spark. And thus all are related: the blacks, the reds, the whites, the browns and all mixtures thereof.

"We are all Africans. With these four words, we see a genetic coalescence of the entire human population. We now know that we descended from the inhabitants of Africa who began migrating out of Africa around 60,000 years ago. In this way, it is impossible for us to not all be, in some way, related.

"In 'Mapping Human History,' Steve Olson has traced the history of our species over the last 100,000 years. With the aid of a computer scientist, a statistician, and a supercomputer, Olson has calculated that we have to go back in time only 2000 to 5000 years to find someone who could count every person on Earth today a direct descendant.

If we go back a little further, 5000 to 7000 years, every person is a direct ancestor to the over six billion people alive today (unless their line of descendancy died out).

"When you walk through an exhibit of Ancient Egyptian art from the time of the pyramids, everything there was likely created by one of your ancestors—every statue, every hieroglyph, every gold necklace. If there is a mummy lying in the center of the room, that person was almost certainly your ancestor, too. It means when Muslims, Jews, or Christians claim to be the children of Abraham, they are all bound to be right.

"No matter the language we speak or the color of our skin, we share ancestors who planted rice on the Yangtze, who first domesticated horses on the steppes of the Ukraine, who hunted giant sloths in the forest of North and South America, and who labored to build the Great Pyramid of Khufu," Olsen and his colleagues wrote in the journal Nature (2006).

When one ponders that we are all Africans, he wonders how white supremacists would react upon being informed that their ancestors evolved in the heart of Africa and migrated to Europe and other continents. Aryans from Africa? What blasphemous nonsense. Eskimos from Africa? Jesus an African? Most of the world doesn't even know of Darwin and Steve Olson and their theories. And if most did, few would believe them.

The world has evolved into a patchwork of tribes, states and nations, all with different languages or dialects and all worshipping one of the four largest religions or one of the 10,000 sects within the four religions. But there have been movements, and the creation of institutions, toward eliminating geographic boundaries, language barriers and religious differences: to wit, the United Nations, the European Union and various national agreements around the globe, attesting to humankind's dream of One World.

But there are proponents and opponents of One World. President Obama is a One Worlder. He believes in diplomacy with other nations and not saber rattling and war, war, war. His opponents believe he is weak and advocate an Al Capone stance: "You will get further with a kind word and a gun than with a kind word." Or Cheney's "It's better to be feared than loved." To the opponents, proponents say that the preceding president was tough and aggressive and thus alienated most of the major countries of world.

Fate may have in store either One World or no world for humankind. Thus, it's time that humans set to work to have it taught everywhere to children that they are all kin, that they all have a common ancestor and that humans are a large family encompassing people from the Arctic to Antarctica, from California to Kamchatka, from Chile to New Zealand. And that it is in the vital interest of every child to see every other child as kin instead of some strange and foreign alien to be feared.

It's idealistic nonsense even to contemplate One World, when one considers the divisions, divisiveness and hostility that are rank among the world's people now. How can one imagine that one day East and West will have resolved their political, economic and religious differences? But what can one do but work toward the resolution of their differences? If ever there is to be a Heaven, humankind will have to create it. So teach that all children have the same father and mother if one goes back far enough into the ancestry of human beings. It may help to bind the billions everywhere that have their beginnings in Africa.

The likelihood that there is a Paradise awaiting good humans and a Hell awaiting bad humans is as probable as that the sun stopped for Joshua or the sea parted for Moses. Paradise, if there is to be one, will be built by the species that has dominated the earth and has in its kindred hands the option of building it here or dying in a Hell of its own making.

Christ's Call from the Cross

ANYONE SEEKING A MORAL MENTOR who happens to discover the story of a man guilty only of teaching beatitudes, who in the agony of his crucifixion calls to God to forgive his tormentors for they know not what they do, must pause and consider whether or not his quest is over. And whether or not there is in the history of man any other person so morally mature that he could, while suffering the intolerable pain of dying on a cross and the despairing depression of unwarranted execution, forgive his executioners. My quest has turned up no such other person. Thus, I consider this story, whether fact or fiction, to present to man the ultimate moral challenge and the ethical sine qua non of peace on earth.

So it was with some discomfort that I read a Rabbi's article titled "Father, forgive them not [sic] for they know what they do," in which he relates that during the Easter week his hearing the Christian message and thinking of the horrendous and heinous acts of the Nazis, Rwandans, Serbs and slave traders assaulted his morning tranquility, arrested his thoughts and impinged upon his very soul. And to soothe his disquiet he remembered a comment made by Elie Wiesel uttered at the 50th anniversary of the liberation or Auschwitz: "God of forgiveness, do not forgive those murderers of Jewish children here."

After reviewing man's inhumanity to man, the Rabbi concludes: "Even God must refrain from issuing blanket forgiveness, especially to so many who abused his precious gift of free will by perverting it into acts of inhuman depravity."

Thus, one learns that the premise of the Rabbi's call upon God to be unforgiving to the morally depraved is their perversion of free will; that is, that they had a free choice to do or not to do what they did. This is a sandy ground upon which to stand in judgment of others and upon which to stand to call to God to act as men act and to be vindictive as men are vindictive.

My first thought upon reading his premise was Spinoza, the Jewish philosopher, who was excommunicated by the Jews for his heretical thinking and conclusions, one of which was that man has no free will, that free will is an illusion and that the understanding that it is an illusion helps man to forgive the depravity of others whether or not he is a victim of the depravity. Every effect has a cause and every cause has an effect, ad infinitum, in physics and in humanity, concluded Spinoza. Since Spinoza cannot be refuted, the premise of free will is suspect.

The more man learns of life–and God knows man is probing relentlessly into the mysteries of it all–the more evidence he discovers that man's will is not free, that free will is, in fact, an illusion, and that man is a product of nature and nurture, neither of which is the free choice of anyone. But just as man cannot live without creating a God in his image, so he cannot abide the thought that he is determined.

"We have no right to forgive the murderers of innocents," writes Levi's successor. Who is innocent? Every society has the criminals it deserves and deserves the crimes committed against it, observed Havelock Ellis. One surveying history and the present, finds no end of evidence to corroborate Ellis's observation. Andre Sakharov believed that no man is innocent of the crime of the criminal who appears at the bar of justice to answer for his wrongdoing. And a little introspection and imagination corroborates Sakharov's conclusion. No man is an island unto himself; everyone is part of the main.

Further, the Rabbi premises a God, an entity to whom he addresses himself with some faith that that God hears him. What evidence does he have that out there somewhere is an omniscient entity in the image of man who has bestowed upon mankind free will and when man perverts it, that entity, saith the Rabbi, is "powerless" and is a "victim of his own generosity and his own gifts to mankind?" This is soaring rhetoric winded more with poetry than truth.

"'Forgive and forget' is a glib escape from reality," opines the Rabbi. "Our first and foremost obligation is to remember and to honor the victims of every cruelty, the martyrs of every human depravity. Memory is the catalyst to good works in an effort to preclude history's past atrocities."

"Remember and forgive" may be dubbed glib as well, but it is the better glibness. The Serbs have never forgotten their defeat at Kossovo in 1389 and they have not forgiven either their subsequent 300 years of servitude and humiliations. On the contrary, they have nursed for centuries their memories of the atrocities committed against them into monsters and when the opportunity came to avenge themselves they fell upon the relatively innocent with a ferocity and fierceness incredible to those not nurtured on the milk of retaliation or the ethic of eye-for-an-eye.

The tit for tat, the bomb for bomb, the unforgiveness and deliberate vengeance on both sides are a formula for many more generations of killing exchanges between the Jews and Arabs in the so-called Holy Land. The obviousness that violence begets violence has never in history deterred man from rapine and pillage in retaliation or has any other recourse entered his mind, until the call from the Cross.

The Rabbi writes of the arrogance of those not victims asking forgiveness for perpetrators of mass murders and he describes as "hutzpah" a perpetrator who seeks forgiveness and a mitigation of punishment. But I observe with some trepidation that a member of a tribe that claims to be God's chosen tribe over all other tribes and to have received in stone from God a conveyance of a particular portion of the earth to possess in perpetuity, its heirs, successors and assigns, should feel some inhibition with regard to the use of the words arrogance and hutzpah.

Leo Tolstoy in his "the Gospels in Brief" paraphrases Christ on the issue of judging and forgiving: "You cannot judge, for men are all blind and do not see the truth. ... Those who judge, and condemn others to violent treatment, wounds, and mutilation, or death, wish to correct them, but what can come of their teaching except that the pupils will learn to become just like the teacher? ... However men may wrong you, do not return evil, do not judge or go to law, do not sue and do not punish."

Why Birds Leave the Nest When they Do

A PHOEBE BUILT A NEST on top of the level part of an S-section of a downspout on my daughter's house. The bird had to fly over the deck in order to arrive at the nest so that anyone on the deck had full view of the nest and the bird's mothering. She has raised two broods since early spring, the last of her babies decided to face the world while my daughter and I were having dinner on the deck on the last day of June.

Prior to leaving the nest, the last and number six of the fledglings sat rigidly upright in the nest looking in the direction his five siblings had flown one by one earlier in the day. While we ate I would cast a glance at the bird wondering what he was thinking. There he was alone: no sign of his mother or father about or of any of his brothers and sisters to cheer him on or to congratulate him on graduation day. No one to say: "Go ahead, Junior, spring off and try your wings. They will work."

Junior obviously was not so sure; for he sat without motion for nearly an hour staring straight ahead and contemplating the big moment and, no doubt, pondering whether or not when he did spring off his wings would work. I was so empathetic that I felt a little of that uneasiness and flutter in the midsection that I have felt just before making a talk before my peers or approaching with a gift the love of my life.

While I was taking a mouthful of ham-and-cheese quiche, he left the nest. I missed seeing his flight into the future, nor did I hear it. But my daughter heard it and said to me, "The bird is gone; I just heard it fly away." I was disappointed. I wanted to see the big moment. But a few minutes later my daughter pointed to the porch roof some ten yards away and there was the newcomer to the world ruffling his feathers and stretching his wings. Just as I focused on him, he lifted off into flight with professional poise and ease and disappeared into the trees.

Later while we were walking, my daughter asked me, "Daddy, what tells a bird it's time to leave the nest?" Good question, the answer to which would probably not only inform her what tells a birds its time to fly but what tells all species, including homo sapiens, when its time to do most things. For lack of a better answer, I said that it was like a clock on a washer. The clock is pre-set and as it clicks off minutes, it initiates certain cycles of the washer until the clothes are washed, rinsed and partially dried and then its goes off.

So it is with a bird. Nature pre-sets the bird's clock at conception and when the clock comes to the time to leave the nest the bird leaves the nest; when the clock says catch flies it catches flies; when it says go south or north off it goes; when it says mate it mates; says lay eggs it lays eggs, sits on them, feeds the babes and starts the cycle all over again. And at the time of death, it dies.

When a man sees a sexy woman he doesn't say to himself she is a sexy woman so I am going to will to desire her. He sees her and desires her. A pregnant woman doesn't say it's time to give birth so I'll give birth. Nature pre-sets the clock that says it is time. A boy of eight doesn't say he is ready to be a man and then comes puberty. He must wait until nature's clock ticks the time. Then, he grows hair above his lip, his shoulders broaden, etc. And little girls become women whether they wish to or not and the time of the change is not their choice.

Nature's genome is the washer's clock. Humans are pre-set at conception. One scientist went so far as to say that conception was like the click of a camera, the resulting photo or new being would be at those moments determined with the exception of touching up of the picture and of nurturing of the new being. The more scientists learn about the human genome and the signals emitted by genes the more they lean to nature instead of nurture as the predominant factor in what a person becomes.

In biology I learned that ontogeny recapitulates phylogeny[3]; that is the development of the individual from egg to adult is a repeat of the evolutionary development of the species in which eons of evolution are repeated in the womb, knowledge of which awakened within me no end of speculations. Not only is this true physically, I deduced, but it is true psychologically. For instance, we know that individuals reach intellectual maturity in the teens just as the species reached its intellectual maturity when the brain evolved to its maximum. Thus, by induction, noting the conversions of libertines to contrite Christians between the ages of thirty and fifty, I speculated that humans' moral IQ matured in the evolutionary progression after sexual and intellectual maturity and last among human psychological characteristics. Thus, I dubbed the progression Cell to Saint.

Anatomy is destiny, someone observed. Watching people all my life has convinced me that there is truth in it. There is no amount of nurture that would have morphed the nature of Mike Tyson into a librarian or Marilyn Monroe into a home ec.

---

3 Editor's note—Perry Mann discovered after this essay was published that ontogeny recapitulates phylogeny has been challenged. He noted that Ernst Mayr wrote in <u>What Evolution Is</u>: "What is recapitulated are always particular structures, but never the whole adult form of the ancestor" So there is recapitulation but not the whole adult form.

teacher. The future roles in society of the high school quarter-back and the shapeliest cheerleader are predictable.

Spinoza, a Jew who decided to dedicate his life to the study of man and nature, concluded among other concepts that man's belief that he has a free will is an illusion. It all had a start, says Spinoza, and from that start it was, and is, all cause and effect, ad infinitum. No decision is free. Every decision is weighted with the whole history of life. Every decision, just as the Phoebe's to fly, had its origin in nature's pre-set clock.

Man watches other species and notes they are programmed. That they have built in them clocks that signal when they are to mate, fly south, sing their territorial songs, and come together in defense against common enemies. He laughs at the notion that he too is programmed; for he has this grand presumption that he is god-like and that he has been created in the image of God.

Thus, I watch the Phoebes as a God watches us and see that they do as their pre-set clock dictates; I study the accounts of the reading of the genome and perceive that nature has over millions of years programmed man; I see that a human's physique determines somewhat his or her destiny; I study in biology that the individual's development repeats the evolution of the species; and I read Spinoza to learn that he concluded that man is no more free to will his destiny than is the Phoebe.

Recently I read that studies have shown that man and woman are not hard-wired to react the same to stress: studies that conclude that man's tendency under stress to fight or flight is not woman's reaction. Hers is to tend and befriend. It seems that under stress the body pumps a great many hormones into our system, including oxytocin, a hormone promoting calm and an inclination toward social interaction. It is secreted in both sexes, but in males under stress testosterone suppresses oxytocin and the tendency to tend and befriend, while in the females estrogen encourages higher levels of oxytocin and induces females to reach out to others for friendship and to support members of the family rather than to fight or to flight.

Surely, the evidence is mounting that what we are and what we do and when we do it are predetermined and that man like a bird has a clock or genome that is set at birth and as it clicks the hours, days and years man reacts to its dictates, believing that his reactions are willed freely.

If Spinoza is right and free will is an illusion or even if there is the possibility that he was right, then, man should consider the premise and the adjustments in morals and laws mandated by it. If one presumes free will as an illusion, he can with a little imagination and cogitation conjure up the enormity of injustice and unfairness perpetrated by man upon man on the holy premise of accountability.

From man's vantage point it is clear to him that a bird leaves the nest when the clock ticks leave; from a god's view of man, it is probably clear to her that what a man does next is written on the wall of the future before he does it.

A Secular Resurrection

MASADA, ISRAEL, OCCUPIES THE ENTIRE top of an isolated mesa near the southwest coast of the Dead Sea. The rhomboid-shaped mountain towers 1,424 feet above the level of the Dead Sea. It has a summit area of about 18 acres. Herod the Great, who was king of Judea under Roman rule and reigned 37-4 BC, made it a royal citadel. His constructions included two ornate palaces, defensive towers, heavy walls, and aqueducts that brought water to cisterns holding nearly 200,000 gallons.

Following the fall of Jerusalem and the destruction of the Second Temple (AD 70), the Masada garrison—the last remnant of Jewish rule in Palestine—refused to surrender and was besieged by a Roman Legion under Flavius Silva. Masada's unequaled defensive site baffled even the Romans' highly developed siegecraft for a time. It took the Roman army of almost 15,000, fighting a defending force of less than 1,000, including women and children, almost two years to subdue the fortress.

The besiegers built a sloping ramp of earth and stones to bring the soldiers within reach of the stronghold, which fell only after the Romans created a breach in the defenders' walls. The Zealots, however, preferred death to enslavement, and the conquerors found that the defenders had taken their own lives. Only two women and five children—who had hidden in a water conduit—survived to tell the tale.

Herod the Great was the Herod who was ruling at the time of Jesus' birth and who ordered the massacre of the Innocents. He adorned most of his cities, especially Jerusalem and he undoubtedly ordered that date palms be planted from one end of Palestine to the other. Somewhere near Masada, one of those date palms—about the time that Christ was born or probably about the time the Masada garrison chose death instead of surrender —dropped a fertile date that was harvested and stored. It remained stored for two thousand years during which time much happened. Among the happenings were:

Jesus was born in Bethlehem in a manger to Mary and Joseph, not many years after Julius Caesar was assassinated. Jesus himself was crucified some thirty years later. In 306 Constantine became Emperor of Rome, the first Emperor to have acknowledged Jesus as the Son of God. In 337 he was baptized on his death-bed. In 410 the Roman Empire shuddered as the Visigoths under Alaric captured Rome.

In 570 Muhammad was born and he died in 632. During his lifetime he established a religion and set about spreading it while conquering a good part of his world. His death resulted in a schism, a schism that is alive today causing the killing of Shiites by Sunnis and Sunnis by Shiites. His successors carried Islam to the gates of Paris where Charles Martel in 732 defeated the Moslems at Poitiers.

The palm date was still dormant in 1066 when William the Conqueror defeated Harold Harefoot at Hastings, which changed the world, particularly the English language. There is now in the English language a French word and an equivalent Anglo-Saxon word for every thing and every thought and concept.

In 1453 the Ottoman Turks under Muhammad II captured Constantinople, a city named after the first Christian Roman Emperor. Just twenty years later Copernicus was born, a birth that was to revolutionize the way man saw himself. Before Copernicus earth was the center of the universe and on it resided God's children. After Copernicus humankind was a species among many species spinning in space among an infinity of other celestial bodies.

In 1492 Columbus discovered America. 1564 Shakespeare was born. In 1643 Louis XIV began a reign of 72 years. In 1789 the Bastille was stormed and the French Revolution began. In 1815, Napoleon was defeated at Waterloo. In 1865 General Robert E. Lee surrendered at Appomattox Court House, ending the Civil War. Life went on.

On January 25, 2005, a seed discovered in the desert fortress of Masada, which by Carbon dating was shown to be 2,000 years old, was planted in sterile soil. On March 3, 2005, the soil cracked and a shoot later appeared. It was a fledgling date palm. "The first leaves were discolored and white, but those that grew later were a normal green. Today the seedling is about three feet high, with a short inner shoot and delicate fronds."

From the days of Herod the Great to the days of George the Weak, for two thousand years, the embryo in that date seed lay alive waiting for a confluence of soil, water and sun in order to flower and flourish. Here is how it happened.

On a sunny day under Herod's reign a flower burst open on the date palm and pollen touched the stigma producing a pregnant ovary. The pregnant ovary remained alive and fertile for twenty centuries without sustenance or company or anything but the hope of conditions that would allow it to flower. Then the conditions came and it flowered. A date palm in limbo for eons finally stretched its legs, raised its arms and sat up, so to speak, after a Sleep of Hundreds of Generations.

Christ lay in his tomb for a day and a night before he rose. The date seed lay in its tomb two thousand years before its secular resurrection. The date's resurrection is not clouded with mystery and question as is Christ's. The miracle of the date is a fact. Nature has out-miracled religion.

Jane Goodall, primatologist, reports in SIERRA, May/June 2013, that the date seed and tree described herein thrived and is thriving. It is known as Methuselah

"The Fierce Urgency of Now"

"WILL WE POWER DOWN AND follow the pathway to sustainability? Or keep on the road of supposedly never-ending growth in numbers of people and amount of stuff consumed. It seems to me that today's economic cataclysm has already exposed the dead end of that road.

"If we want to live sustainably and peacefully, we have to get serious about confronting the overpopulation problem. We are still adding 80 million people to the planet each year. And millions of people are on the move, the greatest number in history, destabilizing both social and environmental systems." *Marilyn Hempel. From her editorial in "Population Press" 2008.*

The current economic cataclysm has accentuated the world's global dilemma with emphasis in China and United States whose economies are already environmentally unsustainable and where, in order to have full employment and economic growth, further unsustainability is not only the heart of the plans of recovery but the soul and history of expedient capitalism. That is, for capitalism to flourish and profit, it must rape the environment for resources, produce stuff in abundance, pollute the air and dirty the streams in the process and encourage people to procreate in order to have more people to buy the stuff, all of which is a scenario for disaster—because it's unsustainable. Unsustainability results when the earth can no longer sustain the population. Haiti, Afghanistan and Malawi are examples of it.

An Ecological Footprint is the acreage it takes to sustain an individual's lifestyle. In the United States its takes 24 acres per capita, the highest in the world. In Europe 12 acres and in Haiti one acre. Humanity's Ecological Footprints in 2005 exceeded the earth's capacity to produce the resources by 31%. That is, it takes a year and three months for the earth to regenerate what humans use in a single year. "Humanity is living off its ecological credit card. While this can be done for a short while, overshoot (ecological debt) ultimately leads to liquidation of the planet's ecological assets, and the depletion of resources, such as forests, oceans, and agricultural land upon which our economy depends." It's estimated that at the present rate of population growth by 2040 it will take two planets to meet humanity's demands.

China and the U.S. each require 21% of global biocapacity— together almost half of all human demand on nature's services. The U.S. is obscenely prodigal in its demand on nature and has been and will be apparently until the liquidation of nature itself. This nation's addiction to stuff and things, to the automobile, mansions, to a hedonism that would have caused Solomon to ache with envy, apparently can be kicked only by a clout on the snout, that is, by the rudest and most grievous sort of awakening to the results of ecological bankruptcy.

The clout on the snout may come as a result of global warming, a phenomenon exacerbated by humanities' carbon footprints, which are one half of its Ecological Footprints. Greenland's glaciers are melting. The Illulissat glacier is spawning icebergs at the rate of 20 million tons of ice per day. It is estimated that it is its smallest in 6000 years. It is calculated that Greenland's glaciers will this year slide about 52.7 cubic miles of ice into the sea, contributing to a rise in sea level worldwide.

The melting glaciers in Greenland are sinking the islands in the Pacific. The islanders of Tuvalu, nine tiny Pacific islands that are a group of tropical atolls and reefs just two meters above sea level, are losing their land to sea water. They are looking for a place to go to resettle their 12,000 islanders.

In Holland ice skating is a mostly a memory. The winters are warmer. The threat of climate change has caused Hollanders to take their fingers from the dikes that have held back the sea for nearly 400 years and allow the sea to have land that is in places 22 feet below sea level. But, now they are working to live on the sea in floating homes and to cultivate floating greenhouses for food. In the Netherlands the handwriting is on the wall: The Sea is coming.

The fierce urgency of now is to recognize that humanity is on the Titanic. The iceberg is the mindless procreation of more people, the prodigal use of earth's resources, the creation and frenetic consumption of stuff, the mal-distribution of wealth, the daily indignity of dumping tons of trash and the maintenance of an economic system, the implementation of whose dogmas build a bigger iceberg day by day.

Where are the leaders in the world who cry Enough?! Enough population! Enough maniacal consumerism! Enough reinless capitalism! Enough of rank wealth juxtaposed to abject poverty! And enough of the species Homo sapiens —one of 10 million species—monopolizing the earth to an extent that the others are threatened with extinction!!!

And where are the pro-life religionists who consider every human, alive or conceived, holy and who thus oppose contraception, abortion and euthanasia—while the ship of Humanity, on its present course, is doomed? No god that views what mankind has done with this planet would excuse it or consider providing another or a Heaven for that species that is creating a Hell.

The Ecstasies and Agonies
of My Political Life

"IF THERE IS ANYONE OUT there who still doubts America is a place where all things are possible, who still wonders if the dream of our founders is alive in our time, who still questions the power of our democracy, tonight is your answer." From Barack Obama's acceptance speech, November 5, 2008.

I have been a doubter for a long time particularly during the last eight years. But no longer. The election of Barack Obama is the fulfillment of my political dreams. It is because not only is he a black American, but he is a liberal, an intellectual and an articulate statesman. I never dreamed it could happen particularly in my lifetime. But it has. I have the additional joy of knowing that my grandson, who is biracial, will never know, except through the reading of history, the harsh discrimination his ancestors on his father's side endured for centuries.

I voted in October, 1944, for the first time for FDR by flashlight in a bombed building on the outskirts of Tunis, Tunisia. And as a result of FDR's GI Bill, I was able to acquire three degrees from prestigious universities. The education has made all the difference in my economic, social, and intellectual life. I remember, while stationed at an airfield in the Sahara desert, being told in April, 1945, that FDR had died

I was politically mature enough to enjoy the exhilaration upon reading The Chicago Tribune's headline claiming unequivocally that Thomas Dewey had defeated Harry Truman for the presidency in 1948—when in fact Truman had won. I also remember with satisfaction that Truman relieved General Douglas MacArthur from command of the American forces in Korea for arrogance. I remember as well when MacArthur returned like Caesar to speak before the Congress and expressed the observation "Old soldiers never die; they just fade away."

Then Adlai Stevenson came upon the political scene. I was immediately ready to crown him king. Here was a man who was liberal, intelligent, articulate, and a Democrat with impeccable credentials and a winning personality. How could America not elect such an outstanding candidate? But it did, twice. Cynicism entered my young soul. I couldn't believe that an electorate could pass the chance to elect such a man to the presidency. Not once but twice, I kept saying to myself. Eisenhower's greatest contribution was to warn the nation of the threat of a military-industrial complex. His worst was to choose Richard Nixon as his running mate.

When Richard Nixon appeared on the stage, I recoiled not only at his appearance and demeanor but his politics. How could Ike ever have selected him as vice-president? When he lost to John Kennedy, the victory for me was doubly joyous: Nixon was defeated, and Kennedy was elected in spite of his religion, and West Virginia had voted for him. This was ecstasy.

I remember the moment that I learned that John Kennedy had been assassinated in Dallas. It was agony to believe it. Such an Apollo! Such a handsome and intelligent and compassionate soul killed by an outcast! America reached near its nadir.

Lyndon Johnson restored my faith to some extent when he advocated and had passed the civil rights act that gave the vote irrevocably to blacks and implemented the legislation. But I lost that bit of faith when he decided to stop communism in Viet Nam, sent thousands to their death, both Americans and Vietnamese, and scorched the earth of that poor country.

Lyndon Johnson alienated the Dixiecrats with his civil rights legislation, and they changed parties. The change helped Richard Nixon to win the presidency. He defeated in 1968 Hubert Humphrey, a happy liberal, and he defeated soundly George McGovern, a WWII hero, in 1972. I questioned the electorate's intelligence, knowledge, and common sense. My judgment that it had made the wrong choice was vindicated when Nixon waved goodbye, boarded a helicopter, and left a political paraplegic, if not a crook.

Carter had a heart larger than his cerebrum, and in the world of politics one must not listen to Christ but to Machiavelli. Thus, he did not gain a second term. Instead he lost to Ronald Reagan as a result of the Iranian debacle.

When Reagan pronounced pontifically that government is the problem, not the solution, I said this man is not my president. I did so because I thought of FDR and his government. He and it rescued capitalism from its cupidity and its myopic ideology and defeated the most sinister and powerful fascist threat to this nation's democratic existence since its inception. The defeat of the Japanese Empire and the Nazis was a governmental solution.

Bush I set a poor example for his son when he decided that Hussein's invasion of Kuwait could not stand. This was a decision engendered not so much from morals as it was from oil. At least, he had the sense to defeat Hussein and leave.

I voted for Clinton and Gore and rejoiced over their election. I expected Clinton to win over Dole and he did. Clinton's extramarital episodes tarnished his administration, but Republican self-righteousness, hypocrisy, and vengeful fanaticism countervailed his peccadilloes.

The choice of George W. Bush as a candidate for the presidency by the Republicans was appalling enough, but for this country to have elected him, not once but twice, made me long for Canada as a sanctuary until the country had regained its sanity. And I was right from day one. I wrote that he was corporate creature, birthed by it, sustained by it, and used by it. And so it happened, and the results are the disaster that Obama will have to deal with. "Tonight is your answer." I thank the fates that be for this victory. At last this nation has demonstrated indubitably that it is ready to accept as its leader a black American who is an intellectual and an elite in that he has the mind, intelligence, and education well above the average American. May he use them to rescue this nation from its nearly unprecedented problems and thereby exile neoconservatives to the wilderness for the remainder of the century.

Gleanings from Years of Reading

UNTIL I WAS TWENTY I could count on my fingers the books I had read. I caught on fire to read in WWII, and the blaze has raged for years and still burns. I have read hundreds of books mostly classics, and I have most of them cased, still. What have I gained and learned from all this eye effort that has made it worthwhile? Read on and discover what I have learned and how it has helped me to live a long and enjoyable life.

From my earliest days my parents, my grandparents, and preachers indoctrinated me with Christian dogma. They brainwashed me, but it didn't take. Why? Because my genes resisted the indoctrination. I have learned that Creationism is a myth, just as are the religions of the Greek and Romans and all other religions from time out of mind.

From Charles Darwin and many others, I learned that humans and all other life on this earth evolved from an original organism. Thus, I am not enthralled by senseless dogma. I revere, appreciate, and respect my species and all others on the basis that they are related to me; upon their health, my health is dependent.

From my reading, I believe that the mind is not a blank slate upon which the senses write and thus determine the mindset of one. There is built into the genes the history of mankind, and that history to a large extent determines everyone's mindset. Conscience is not acquired; it is built in. As a boy cutting hay with a horse-drawn mower, I cut over a quail's nest. From the nest scurried a dozen wee chicks. The mother quail instead of fleeing remained and acted as if her wing was impaired. But when I approached her she flew, leading me away from her offspring. Thus, there is in a bird responsibility and conscience.

Consciousness is not a transcendent entity. It is as much a part of the material body as is the brain from which it springs. If an electric current flows through a coil of wire, an electromagnetic field of force is created, a force that is measurable. When the current stops flowing the field collapses. Likewise, when the brain dies, consciousness dies.

Descarte, the great French philosopher, postulated that humankind was dual, a body and a soul. He agreed with church dogma that the soul is eternal and has an afterlife whether in hell or in heaven determined by more church dogma. The soul is no more than consciousness and is just as mortal.

Humankind believes that it has free will. The illusion is so strong that few believe that they do not choose freely the decisions they make. But the truth in a nutshell probably is that every act of mankind is the result of all the circumstances and influence that have impinged upon life since life began four billion years ago. If one considers to a large extent he is what his genes dictate and what his environment fashions, he can reasonably suspect he has no free will and his acts are determined by the totality of the history of life.

From Henry George, I ascertained often the increase in the value of one's unimproved land is the result of the work of others and the appreciation should be taxed heavily, if not confiscated, for the benefit of all the people. From him I perceived that the chief reason for great wealth juxtaposed with extreme poverty is the monopoly of land and the rise of rent, without further improvements, upon a greater demand for the use of the land, a demand often created by capital and labor.

Karl Marx taught me that profit is that value labor produces but is expropriated by capital. Therein is the basis for the conflict and class war between capital and labor. Capital wants cheap labor in order to have more profits, and labor wants high wages in order to live other than from one payday to another. I also learned of the alienation labor suffers. The assembly line is a hellish arrangement for labor and heavenly for capital.

From the great British historian Arnold Toynbee, I discovered the concept "The Nemesis of Creativity." That nemesis causes subsequent failure. Nothing fails like success in the long run. It's akin to one of Christ's Beatitudes: The meek inherit the earth. The concept is at work in this nation, to wit: Iraq.

From the great English poet William Blake, I learned from just four of his poetic lines that possession kills. That to possess is to depreciate the possession. And that to possess obsessively in passionate love—kills it quick. His advice was to kiss the joy on the fly.

Thus, I believe that consciousness is an aspect of the material world just as is everything else. I am a monist and not a dualist; that is, I do not believe man has a soul or that there is a hereafter for it to exist eternally. Therefore, I do the best I can to enjoy this life and to protect and revere nature, the mother of us all, and to help others to the enjoyment of it.

I doubt that humans have free will. Thus, I question the criminal system that operates on the principle revenge is the proper response to crime. Further, I have an easier time forgiving the crimes and torts committed by people—even those I suffer.

I deplore an economic system that allows one to buy cheap and sell dear and pay minimal taxes. And I deplore a system that expropriates the surplus value created by labor and moves capital to foreign lands to escape paying a fair wage to organized workers.

I rejoice in nature, its beauties, its miracles, and the tranquility it brings in contemplation of it. And I rejoice in the arts which are reflections of it.

The Last Illusion

"A DUALIST ACKNOWLEDGES A FUNDAMENTAL distinction between matter and mind. A monist, by contrast, believes mind is a manifestation of matter…and cannot exist apart from matter." from "The God Delusion" by Richard Dawkins

My mother, like her mother, told her children Bible stories with a view to bringing them up right. I remember being told of Noah building the Ark to save the good people and animals from the forty days and forty nights of rain. I recall one night during a dreadful rainstorm calling to my mother for reassurances that another such flood would not come. At other times, she cautioned me that I should be good because God sat on a throne in Heaven and kept books on everyone, recording daily good deeds and bad deeds, for a final reckoning on Judgment Day, when God determined who would go to Heaven and who would go to Hell.

Parents, ages ago, taught their offspring that the earth was flat. And learned professors in more enlightened times taught that the earth was the center around which all celestial bodies moved including the sun. But Magellan, once and for all, disproved the flat-earth theory; and Copernicus, much to the chagrin of the church, announced that the earth circled the sun and that the earth was not the center of the universe. Galileo nearly lost his life in support of Copernicus's heresy.

And, of course, I believed in Santa Claus and the story that he traveled on Christmas night with a deer-drawn sleigh loaded with presents for good boys and girls, came down the chimney, deposited the presents under the Christmas tree, ate the cookies set out for him and with a ho, ho, took off to visit the next family. Also, in the tooth fairy and the Easter bunny.

Without doubt, the strongest belief I ever had was that I would love my first love forever. I cannot stress how certain I was that she was the only being in all the world that would insure that I would always be ecstatically happy so long as she loved me with the fidelity that angels love God.

But woe was me when whatever erodes love eroded my love and left me stranded naked in existence, painfully puzzled, and suddenly unanchored and adrift, much as is the condition of a spider whose web is swept away by an earthly and unimaginative housekeeper.

Where was one to look to find a foundation upon which to build a house of happiness that would withstand all erosions and disillusionments? I turned again to Christianity. I turned mostly to the ineffable morals of the Sermon on the Mount and to the Author thereof. But I soon learned that his message was subordinate to the church's concern with liturgy, with ritual and with maintenance of the supernatural aspect of its theology. It was a dead end, except for the Sermon.

Knowledge was next. After an introduction to the liberal arts while earning a BA degree, I learned that scholars had agreed on 100 books as the greatest literary achievements of all time. I got the list and I diligently began to read. Becoming addicted to books was one of the smartest things I did in life. There is no end to great books; they are relatively inexpensive, particularly the classics; and reading them does no damage to one's health but does wonderful things for one's mind and spirit. But reading great literature is a Sisyphean endeavor: it's interminable. Yet it was productive in that from my studies I disposed of other illusions and gleaned some truths.

Darwin's theory upended Creationism, a myth anyone who has a curious and critical mind would find entertaining but beyond serious consideration as to the actual creation of man and earth and all the species earth mothers. Evolution is a more exciting, marvelous and believable explanation of how man got here and how he and all his plant and animal relations came to be.

Upon learning that philosophers considered freewill an illusion, I remained somewhat catatonic for days, considering the ramifications of the discovery. My first awareness that there was a controversy between free will and determinism was nearly six decades ago and I have studied the issue since. I am strongly convinced that free will is an illusion; that is, that man's fate is inexorably and inevitably determined. He just has the illusion that he has a free choice. His anthropocentrism feeds the illusion, which induces arrogance and pride and error.

Whether one acts always with self interest above all other interests was an issue I wondered about. I concluded that every act is selfish but that there are acts, even though selfish, that benefit others and there are acts that benefit only the actor and do harm to others. Mark Twain concluded: "From cradle to grave, a man never does a single thing which has any first and foremost object but one—to secure peace of mind, spiritual comfort, for himself."

Now I am reading Daniel Dennett's "Consciousness Explained." His thesis is that consciousness and the brain are one and the same; that is, there is no soul or spirit. There is only the illusion that there is. Just as the sun seems to rise and set, it seems to man that he is dual: mind and soul; but it only seems to him to be so. Man is all cause and effect, all chemical and electrical substance, just a materialistic machine. This is the death of the last illusion, if Dennett's theory is true.

What if it is true that man has no free will and that he has no soul? Even the possibility that he has no free will, is cause enough to indict the criminal system with perpetrating centuries of outrageous and horrendous injustices and continuing them in so-called enlightened times. And if there is the possibility of no soul, the implications of it staggers the mind as to what has come from believing that he does or that he doesn't. There is a vast clerical hierarchy, uncountable free-lance preachers and an infrastructure of churches, cathedrals and monuments that stacked on end would reach to Heaven—that would collapse into irrelevancy, if, in fact, man and woman are soulless; that is, are monistic instead of dualistic.

The very possibilities should be enough to temper faith and belief and induce man to look with passionate care to nature, his mother, for guidance, nurture and spirituality. And for a future.

A Lifetime of Lessons

August 1, 2012

A SUMMARY OF WHAT I have learned and advocate from a life time of living and reading and thinking:

Sexual love is ephemeral. Lasting love is based on ethical, secular and philosophical, political and religious compatibility. Once the excitement of sex is muted, if there is nothing else, it's the end of wedding bliss and just a humdrum day to day thereafter.

Marriage is for children. Without children a marriage is naturally sterile. Nature does its best to bring children but often her best is frustrated, sometimes properly. But always it's a loss to the partners. But, another child in a world crowded with children and their parents eating into Earth's sustainability along with 7 billion other mouths—is a certain and always problem of global concern.

Seek knowledge with a fervor others seek money. Read all the best that has been written, if not all as much of it as life allows you the time to read. There is no safer path to walk than that laid out by those intellectuals and saints that have walked the path and written of those paths to take and those to avoid. And great literature and poetry are sustenance for the spirit.

Eschew religions. They have no foundation in fact. They do harm as history attests. They do some good. But the basis of their beliefs is mythical. Secular humanism is what one should investigate. It is the future. It is based on science and philosophy and the reason and empathy Nature birthed. Also, question the concepts of Heaven and Hell and an eternal soul and much else that are the bases of Christianity.

Free will is an illusion. It has so been declared by minds of great intelligence and scholarship. Even Spinoza, a Jewish philosopher who lived 1632-1677, taught it. The concept allows you to forgive all the atrocities that people do and to understand that greatness is Fated. It is the basis of that aspect of liberalism that is empathy. It is the answer to the revengeful view of conservatives' accountability and responsibility.

Nature is everyone's Mother. To do damage to Her is the ultimate sin. Neither this nation nor any other nation can long survive without the love and care of Mother Nature. Live near her, protect her, and revere her. Do what you do with the understanding that it should be compatible with Nature's welfare and her longevity. For all our lives are dependent on the welfare of Her Life.

Work toward a socialistic but democratic political system. Capitalism is a cancer on Mother Nature. It exploits her for profits unconscionably and disastrously. And then leaves garbage of Mt Everest dimensions for mankind to bury. Also, it begets billionaires. Financial obscenities. And malls where people assault one another over an item of sale: Like animals with no God-given conscience. Socialism would help to take from the PRIVATEERS, who rolled dice and captured wealth, and would redistribute the wealth fairly to those who create it. There is no economic freedom for anyone if there is no Nature to exploit. What are capitalists to do with a dead Nature?

Live near Nature. Avoid the city, the corrupt environment created by mankind as a substitute for Nature's. Live as close as you can with forests, meadows, fields, brooks, streams and all bodies of water, the source of your beginning. And a place where in evening the sun sets before your eyes and at night the heavens are clear and the arc of the stars stuns you for a moment.

Do your best to make your avocation your vocation. Most lives are spent in an occupation they dislike or even hate. No one should have to live that way. But it is not easy to avoid such a life. Never just follow the path of someone close to you that has endured such a life. Capitalism loves those who dress in its harness and pull for the best years of their lives for little while producing much. Don't settle soon for a work that will take you from youth to retirement in work you do not do with enthusiasm and is a work that does damage for profit to Mother Nature.

Tolerate and love all people everywhere. Tolstoy taught that we should love and be kind to all. He taught that all people had one origin and thus were all kin and should be acceptable in a Grand Union or Peoples' Union. He dislike the notion that some were worthy of praise and worship and some were not worthy of a good day's blessing. Read the Sermon on the Mount.

Always remember that the building blocks of nature are miniscule. Remember that all organic and inorganic matter; that is, all life and non-life is reducible to bits of the constituents of the Big Bang, including you.

The Right's belief that without religion humans have no moral guide is nonsense. Anyone close to nature has seen no end of evidence of morality in the animal kingdom. In fact, there would be no animal kingdom or any other kingdom without Nature's built in morality. Conscience is Nature. The mother of every animal watches over her progeny with care and danger to her life. Morality is not Heaven sent but Nature gifted.

Mankind and all else, flesh and rocks, came from the Big Bang billions of years ago. All that has come from it is kin, all life and all non-life. The kinship now is unquestionable.

Mankind and all life have a beginning and end. So mankind has from that basis decided that the Universe has a beginning and end. But that conclusion may be wrong. It may be that the Universe just Is and always has been just Is. No beginning and no end. So it will go on into Eternity.

Stay free of debts. Every dollar of debt is a small shackle on your freedom. Creditors interfere with digestion and sleep.

Finally, but foremost, take care of your health, for if health goes—little else matters.

Home to the Mother

"I SADLY SMILING REMEMBER THAT the flower fades to make fruit, the fruit rots to make earth. Out of the mother; and through the spring exultances, ripeness and decadence; and home to the mother."

The above is from "Shine, Perishing Republic," a poem by Robinson Jeffers (1887-1962), an America poet who never had to work a day for a living and who was a misanthrope, a nature lover and a prescient thinker. He was born into wealth and classical culture. He married and with the help of his twin sons built himself a house of boulders on a height in California, where he immured himself, contemplated man and nature, and wrote into his poetry his ruminations.

I don't know when Jeffers wrote "Shine, Perishing Republic," but it doesn't matter when. What matters to me is how current is the thinking in it. How could America's present be better stated in so few words: "While this America settles in the mold of its vulgarity, heavily thickening to empire, / And protest, only a bubble in the molten mass, pops and sighs out, and the mass hardens,...."

When I grew up in the Thirties this nation was isolationist to the core. The Monroe Doctrine was viable. This country's standing army was a few thousands soldiers, many of whom trained with wooden guns and cardboard tanks. In 1936 at

Langley Field, I saw all of the Army Air Corps' heavy bomber force: seven B-17s. And I saw at Newport News, VA, the just-built aircraft carrier Yorktown, one of the few flat-tops available to the navy and one of a number sunk by Japanese action. America was a republic, inferior in military might to Great Britain, France, Germany, Japan, and perhaps Russia. And even though the times were in the depth of the Depression, there was nothing like the ill distribution of the nation's wealth that is today so conspicuous and divisive.

When war came with Japan and Germany and their allies, every able-bodied youth from farm, factory and university, of common blood or of blueblood, of pallid or red neck, either enlisted or was drafted. It was a citizens' army that fought and died for the democracy that was America in 1941. My two closest prewar buddies, buddies with whom I worked in fields and hunted in woods, sailed to Europe in convoy, marched with other farm boys across the Old World – one of them having helped to take the bridge at Remagen – and were there when the end came. The Greatest Generation was made of everyone, from everywhere, high and low in social status, and the sacrifices were more equitable than, say, in Vietnam.

Then, there was a man in the White House who damned the Robber Barons of old and their successors of his day and talked about equitable distribution of the nation's wealth and social justice, and eyed them with be damned to those who whined that he was promoting class warfare. He curbed the corporcrates and put the bureaucrats to work for the people.

Then came Reagan with his premise that government isn't the solution but the problem and his favoring the wealthy over the poor. Since, America has slowly but surely metamorphosed from democracy, admittedly less than perfect, to a plutocracy, a government of the wealthy, which is ruled by bought politicians and gold-plated corporcrates. And it has so increased the power, so expanded the might of the military, so extended its power around the world that it is on the brink of empire and the rule, not just of the wealthy and the corporcrates, but as well the rule of the protectors of their wealth and power, the military. Thus has been the metamorphosis from bloom to fruit to rot of republics in Athens and Rome and wherever they have risen to power and wealth.

There are grounds for optimism, though. Hear Jeffers: "But for my children, I would have them keep their distance from the thickening center; corruption / Never has been compulsory, when the cities lie at the monster's feet there are left the mountains." And there is where I am and where my children were reared, and it has made all the difference.

I live with one foot in the 21st century and another in the 19th century. My roots are in the land: in planting in spring and harvesting in fall, in preserving the bounty of the earth, walking the fields in April's green birth and in October's golden demise, watching the drama of weather and its storms and serenities, smelling the flowers and hearing the birds and having access to a mountaintop where in day one can see in circle the whole of the horizons and view at night the heavens in full scope with all the starry sights undiluted by man's ubiquitous incandescence. And my children have "keep their distance from the thickening center" of vulgarity and corruption, a blessing unparalleled by any other blessing on earth and probably in heaven.

"You making haste, haste on decay: not blameworthy; life is good, be it stubbornly long or suddenly / A mortal splendor: meteors are not needed less than mountains: shine, perishing republic."

Time is money say the money changers from Christ's day to this day, when all of them squat and role the dice in the columned temples on Wall Street. Haste is a virtue to those who measure virtue by high, low, and close. Society needs those whose careers are meteoric, but it needs as much those who build on rock and endure as the mountains.

And who can argue with Jeffers' advice to his sons: "And boys, be in nothing so moderate as in love of man, a clever servant, insufferable master. There is the trap that catches noblest spirits that caught – they say – God, when he walked the earth."

But there is further reason for optimism amid all the decadence and cynicism. Nature renews and recreates. Barren and worn soil is rejuvenated and made fertile again once man abandons it. And nature does so in every corner of its jurisdiction whether on land or in seas, and throughout the heights and depths and widths of the universe. The law is that sooner are later all goes home to mother to become the seeds and sustenance of future births.

Tributes from Perry Mann's
Son and Daughter

PERRY'S SON JEFF, ASSOCIATE PROFESSOR and Director of the Master of Fine Arts in Creative Writing Program, invited him to speak at Virginia Tech University. Jeff gave this introduction:

My father, Perry Mann, is a lawyer and a farmer. He is also a fine writer, which is, obviously, the point of our gathering here this evening. He's been publishing essays in several West Virginia newspapers for decades, and now, thanks to Ann Farrell Bowers, a former student of his and now the head of Kettle Moraine Publishing, he has published a collection of essays about country living and the environment, *Mann and Nature*, from which he will read tonight.

Rarely have I had the opportunity to introduce a writer who has influenced me as profoundly as my father has. From him I've gotten my dedication to books and literature (witness my English degrees from West Virginia University, my voracious reading, and my own publications), my love of the outdoors (witness my Nature Interpretation degree from the same institution and my compulsive botanizing in poem after poem), my pride in my country roots and the Appalachian culture that has shaped me, my devotion to down-home cooking and strong drink, and my snarly detestation of conservatives and religious fundamentalists. In fact, almost every intellectual or emotional trait I possess—other than my same-sex attraction to hairy men, a mystery no science can yet explain—I can trace to his influence.

On this point, my lusty admiration for men, I should add that not only has my father been hugely understanding, but he's been protective as well, even using his literary abilities to defend me and my queer kind. In the late nineties, my sister Amy called one weekend to ask if I'd seen the latest issue of *The Charleston Gazette*. I had not. "Well" she advised, "you'd better. Daddy published an article about you." Oh, Lord. I tracked a copy of the newspaper down. In it was my father's letter to the editor, "Hatemonger Preachers Could Inspire Violence." Turns out that a Baptist minister in the Kanawha Valley had stated in the *Gazette* that "gays, lesbians, and pedophiles" were not welcome in the Mountain State. Daddy—yes, even at my present age of fifty-two, I still call my father "Daddy"—began his attack on the nasty preacher by proclaiming, "My son is gay. Further, he is not normal. He never has been, nor ever will be." After that statewide outing, I began joking about being "The Official Homosexual of the State of West Virginia," but of course I was hugely grateful for his eloquent words against homophobia. God knows there are many LGBT folks whose families are far less understanding.

Once, in the early eighties, having fallen in love with another in a long line of handsome, callous narcissists, I'd gone into therapy in search of some relief from pain and romantic confusion, my therapist at one point said, "Well, you know the only reason you think the way you do about so many things is because your father has taught you to think that way," I cogitated, then said, with less defensiveness than pure conviction, "That's true. But he's right."

I still think that. He's right about the wholesomeness of country living, he's right about religious conservatives and their virulent hypocrisies, and he's right about the prime importance of nature in our lives. I'm not the only one to think so. He has a wide and enthusiastic readership, not only folks all over West

Virginia, but now, thanks to the Internet, all over the world. He has an enviable collection of fan letters, both e-mailed and hand written. Robert Shetterly, whose portrait of Daddy serves as the cover of *Mann and Nature*, included him, in *Americans Who Tell The Truth*, among such famous figures as Henry David Thoreau and Walt Whitman.

This honor is well deserved. Daddy's been telling his truths, however unpopular they might occasionally be, all his life. He was outspoken in the sixties, when his protests against racist policies in the schools of Covington, Virginia, where he taught at the time, cost him his job. He's been outspoken throughout his writing career, championing liberalism and the environment, and so has racked up a good bit of hate mail along with those many fan letters.

His courage – to be and believe and say what he will. – his defiant Emersonian nonconformity, his freedom from that suffocating small-town constriction, "What will people think?!" his Appalachian self-reliance and his restless desire for knowledge are his greatest legacies.

Thanks to his essays. – those published far and wide, and now these collected in this volume from Kettle Moraine Publishing. – the Mann legacy is one that, fortunately, is not restricted to his family. I am very proud and pleased to share him with you all tonight.

A hand printed note on beautiful stationary from Perry Mann's daughter:

3-12-98

On this your 77th birthday, I celebrate your years, your health, your energy, your garden, your humor, your bread, your wealth, your writing, your intelligence, your good looks, your pie crust, your honesty, your conscience, your fairness, your non-conformity and your strength.

Having you as a father, teacher and friend has been and continues to be the greatest blessing of my life. Thank you.

I love you,

Amy

Please send comments to:
Julian Martin, 1525 Hampton Road, Charleston, WV 25314 or martinjul@aol.com. Comments will be forwarded to Perry Mann.

While they last, Ann Bowers book, Mann and Nature is available for $3 postage to Julian Martin, 1525 Hampton Road, Charleston, WV 25314.

45462520R00118

Made in the USA
Lexington, KY
28 September 2015